PARADISE RECONSIDERED

9/11 & 7/7

reincarnation
and
the lost gospel of Jesus

by

R. E. SLATER

CREST PUBLISHING
LONDON
2006

British Library Cataloguing in Publication Data

A catalogue record for this book is available from the British Library

ISBN-10: 0-9553042-0-2
ISBN-13: 978-0-9553042-0-0

Crest Publishing
BCM Box 1398, London WC1N 3XX

NOTE: The paper used in printing comes from sustainable sources
and is recyclable and biodegradable.

Dedication

To truth,
and the spirit of enquiry that leads towards it;

and to my parents,
dedicated churchgoers both,
who showed me that it was possible
to consider the subject of reincarnation
with an open mind and in the
context of Christianity.

Disclaimer

The following has been written entirely in a personal capacity, and as such is not connected with any organisations to which the author belongs.

Contents

Acknowledgements

My thanks to Pat Saunders for her diligent typing; to the late Rt Revd Hugh Montefiore, who encouraged me to complete a manuscript on the subject of reincarnation; to the Revd Don MacGregor, for his encouragement and comments; to Professor Elliott, for his helpful comments; to Professor John Hick, for his helpful advice; to Dr Hilary Johnson, and her perceptive 'reader'; to Dennis Richards, for helping to show how writing on this subject might be possible in a Christian context, via his thesis on a similar topic; to Professor Hans Kung, for his encouraging writing on the subject, and kind comment. With thanks for the help and facilities provided by the following libraries: Lambeth Palace, Westminster Abbey, King's College, Heythrop College, the Catholic Central, and Dr Williams Library.

Thanks are also due to The Society of Authors as the Literary Representative of the Estate of John Masefield for their kind permission to print an extract from 'A Creed'. Thanks to The Churches' Fellowship for Psychical and Spiritual Studies for consent to write the paragraph included concerning the views expressed in their journal. The Edgar Cayce Foundation have kindly granted consent for readings in Noel Langley's book on reincarnation to be quoted.

The responsibility for the content, however, cannot be laid at the feet of the above who, in most cases, the writer of the Foreword included, have not read the full manuscript, but remains with the author. Apologies for any mistakes or omissions, and it is hoped to remedy these in future editions, all being well.

The numbers in square brackets within the text refer to the Bibliography. The numbers not in square brackets refer to the Notes.

Foreword

Reincarnation hasn't been properly analysed from a Christian theological perspective as far as I know. I'm sure this subject does need a radical look at. It has good resonances of a divine continuum within it, which is well worth exploring.

THE RT REVD MICHAEL BALL
Suffragan Bishop of Jarrow;
Bishop of Truro (1990–97)

Introduction

When death occurs suddenly and randomly, as was the case on September the 11th, 2001, in New York, and July the 7th, 2005, in London, how can there be any opportunity for practical forgiveness and reconciliation between the deceased and their murderers? How can those who caused such multiple deaths compensate those that they had killed? And what about babies and children who die without having had the opportunity to live a full adult life? Is this fair? If they are denied the opportunity to be born again, would this not, perhaps, be a denial of divine justice? Would a 'Just God' deny them a chance to make good in life and, in the former case, to actually demonstrate forgiveness?

Now orthodox Christian tradition currently denies, or tends to deny, the idea of reincarnation as an acceptable concept. However, some Christian traditions, or at least ordinary members of the public who follow them, tend to be less unsympathetic to the idea than others. And I don't just mean liberals, compared to conservatives. Catholics in Britain are substantially more sympathetic than evangelicals, for example. In a 1979 Sociology Department of Surrey opinion poll, 27 per cent of Catholics in England and Wales answered 'true' to the statement: 'Sometimes people, after they die, come back and live in the world again.'

In America, a 1982 Gallup poll showed that 26 per cent of Methodists and 25 per cent of Catholics believed in reincarnation – more than the 23 per cent for adults in the USA as a whole. This particular poll also reported that 21 per cent of Protestants believed in reincarnation. And also in the USA, a recent study found that 15 per cent of Presbyterians active in their church, supported the concept of reincarnation. One book, published in 1997, reported that 'a recent Gallup Poll showed that 72 per cent of Americans believe in reincarnation' which, for one of the highest churchgoing populations in the world, is an incredibly high figure. [18] Furthermore, it seems a great increase compared with the figure reported in 1982, but there may well have been a substantial rise in support in the

1

intervening years. These polling surveys are mentioned not with a view to providing percentages that may be relied on as being applicable today, but more to indicate that a fairly substantial number of Christians have been prepared to indicate their support for this belief or doctrine towards the end of the twentieth century. And it was widely – though not universally – accepted within the traditions of Judaism, in the early days of Christianity.

This topic came more sharply into focus, at least in my own mind, as a result of the disasters of September the 11th, 2001, in the USA, and especially the attacks on the World Trade Centre in New York. The question that arises is: 'Will the people who died on that day, or as the result of other attacks, have the opportunity of returning to this earth?' And will those who died whilst undertaking their suicide missions, be obliged to return to this earth in order to make good the harm they caused and to reconcile themselves with their victims? And what, too, of the innocent civilians killed in the bombings of retaliation – you might say retribution – in Afghanistan? Might not the same questions be posed on their behalf? And now, of course, similar questions arise in respect of the war in Iraq.

In a series of articles entitled 'Reincarnation – Islamic Conceptions', M. H. Abidi, a Muslim scholar, (according to Steven Rosen, in his book *The Reincarnation Controversy*) writes: 'The position adopted by the successive luminaries who followed (the Founder of Islam), was to affirm the belief in reincarnation, but not to propagate it as a teaching for the masses, as the teaching of reincarnation requires a subtle, mental approach.' [56]

What I would like to do in exploring this theme, is to summarise some early Christian and Jewish teachings in favour of reincarnation, and reasons why the concept itself fell out of favour, at least in the West.

Starting with a brief assessment of why the subject is not being widely discussed in church circles at present, there follows an overview of some of the historical 'western' arguments in favour of reincarnation, and the views of influential early Christians will be looked at in more detail. This is followed by a short summary of the Jewish background to the subject. A key Early Church Council – Constantinople – and its context will then be described.

It is sometimes said that the biblical texts that we have today were altered in order to exclude overt references to reincarnation, so an exploration of some of the evidence that may support this allegation is included. However, even if no alterations were made, we still have a number of biblical texts that point towards pre-existence, or reincarnation, and these are looked at in a fair degree of detail.

Moving towards more modern times, critics of the concept of reincarnation in terms of 'western' religious beliefs argue that no mainstream or well-known Christians have supported this concept. In fact a number of Churchmen and theologians have looked sympathetically upon this idea, and their views are examined. The crucially important issue of the environment, including earthquakes is also considered, especially in the light of the events of September the 11th, 2001, and their aftermath, which now may be said to include the 'recent' war in Iraq.

Finally, there is a summing up which looks to the future to explore the benefits there would be for Christianity – and other 'Religions of the Book' – once more taking this issue seriously and putting it back on the religious, and public, agenda.

This book is not designed to be of interest only to academics and theologians. For a start, not enough primary sources are quoted to provide the definitive academic base that they would prefer to see. And certain sources quoted from may be regarded as too unusual or even 'sensational' for some readers' taste. Nevertheless, it is designed as a general overview of a very challenging yet fascinating subject that may not have been attempted in recent times. It is intended to help restart a serious debate on the subject of pre-existence, and reincarnation in such a comprehensive way that a recurrence of the events of September the 11th, 2001, and its violent aftermath – including the events of July the 7th, 2005 – might be discouraged, as the wider consequences of such actions are more properly appreciated.

1

The current view in church circles: the Hoddle saga; cloning versus reincarnation

But if – the reader might reasonably ask – many Christian teachers and thinkers in recent decades and centuries have expressed sympathy for this topic, then why, in these times of enlightened debate and exploration of what faith means, has the subject hardly been discussed in church circles – let alone debated or accepted more widely? Why is it not even on the Churches' agenda?

The answer, at least partly, seems to be 'fear'. Fear of ridicule, fear of being labelled 'non-Christian', despite the fact that many well-known Christians, even those as well known as St Francis of Assisi – described by Pope John Paul II as the Patron Saint of Ecology – are said to have supported the doctrine. [64] Such views were also accepted within some sects and influential groups in Judaism. However many church leaders, especially evangelicals, are ultra cautious lest they be accused of 'pandering to Eastern Religions'.

And what of the secular press, and well-known people who have spoken of their interest in this matter? The best known example of recent times is that of Glen Hoddle. He was National Coach of England's football team in the 1998 World Cup Tournament, and he expressed views about rebirth and disabled people which were widely ridiculed in the Press and Media as being insensitive. As a result of this, he was forced to resign. Now if this is the way that our present Christian, or Judeo-Christian-based culture – at least in Britain – reacts to someone well known in another field of endeavour, commenting, albeit in inadvisedly simplistic terms, on this subject, it well illustrates how an anti-reincarnationist view has permeated all sections of society here. If such a reaction takes place in the secular world, sensationalised by the media, then how much more might a similar reaction occur in church circles, when someone's promising career is directly at risk? Or perhaps even in academia, though John Hick seems to have succeeded. [30] And Hans Kung has indicated that such a position can be supported. [34]

It may be, though, that someone less well known or even unknown, could be in a better position to raise this issue in a serious way, and help to put it, once again, on the Churches' agenda. And that of the other monotheistic religions too. Especially if, as a result, it would help to avoid further unnecessary environmental damage, together with the loss of life that would be incurred in a battle involving nuclear weapons as a method of endeavouring to 'resolve' the crisis in Kashmir, for example. If all the parties concerned, appreciated the consequences of their actions in terms of the practical outcome of a Divine Law of reincarnation, then a nuclear battle should not ensue – much to the relief of the rest of the world.

Now in these days of increasing sympathy towards dialogue between different faiths, in more liberal circles, the average lay-person might be forgiven for thinking that the topic of rebirth too might be on the agenda for discussion, especially if this might help to alleviate interfaith fighting, wars – and rumours of wars. But no; in church circles, even those who are retired do not, with a few notable exceptions, seem to wish risking their reputation by writing on this topic. The power of ridicule can be very great, and bishops, for example, would for the most part be instinctively disinclined to stray too far from the realms of 'politically correct' current orthodoxy. And many priests and vicars are said to be afraid of losing their home and employment if they disagree with their ecclesiastical superiors. One minister said that it was vital to be in conformity with the opinion of his bishop. [1]

But bishops' opinions vary from diocese to diocese, as do those of the local clergy. Researchers writing in a theological journal told of a liberal parish priest in Somerset who said that 'of the doctrinal questions that have been asked of me over the years, reincarnation has been top of the list', whereas evangelical clergy tend to report that they do not come across people who express an interest in such a belief. The authors of this report concluded that this more unsympathetic response was because parishioners sensed that their minister would dismiss the idea out of hand, and thus did not ask questions on the subject. [2]

Yet for those who attempt to unravel the truth of this matter, there are biblical texts that may provide some comfort and reassurance; for example:

> And ye shall know the truth, and the truth shall make you free. (John 8.32)

perhaps also:

> for if this counsel or this work be of men, it will come to nought: But if it be of God, ye cannot overthrow it. (Acts 5.39)

The majority of those who identify with present-day Christian traditions may not even appreciate how much evidence there is to support the concept of rebirth, or reincarnation within their own religious tradition – hence the material in this book. It is not the only writing on the subject, of course, but much of this is written from a more 'New Age', or Californian perspective, and tends not to treat the subject in much depth or sympathy from a Church or Christian point of view.

Academics too, more surprisingly, seem disinclined to tackle the subject, according to one published theologian who wrote to me to say that he knew of no one in the academic world who was currently interested in the subject. However, one serious, influential critique was written by John Hick, though the first version of this work was published more than twenty-five years ago now. [30]

One bishop, the Rt Revd Hugh Montefiore, wrote extensively about the medical evidence for reincarnation, as well as setting out some theological reasons why it could prove acceptable in terms of Christian doctrine; but even though he had many books published on other subjects, he found great difficulty in getting any mainstream church or theological publisher to accept the full manuscript because of the nature of the topic, he told me. Thus it is not surprising that the subject does not get taken seriously in church circles, though opinion polls indicate that a significant minority of churchgoers think that it does deserve to be taken seriously, as previously indicated.

There is the Churches' Fellowship for Psychical and Spiritual Studies, in whose *Quarterly Journal* the subject does get discussed from time to time by individuals who write therein, but even this organisation does not regard the subject of reincarnation as being very central to its concerns. Nevertheless, no less than three articles on the subject were included in the December 2002 edition of its Journal.

Cloning versus reincarnation

Another news story that has possible implications concerning the topic of reincarnation is one concerning the 'cloning' of humans.

Among recent press reports on the subject is one which claimed that, thanks to advances in cloning techniques, human beings will one day be able to reincarnate in their present form. It was suggested that, as the result of such cloning, humans would be able to transmit the contents of their existing brain into a youthful, yet adult version of themselves. This, at least, seemed to be the view of Claude Vorilhon, otherwise known as Rael, the leader of a grou, or cult which believes that human beings were created by aliens. [3]

But what if such a view is based on a misconception concerning the importance of the soul? What if it is the soul which animates a human body, if that is indeed what happens, and that this animation is chosen at a heavenly level, rather than at a human one? Will that not invalidate the stated aim of this, or any other such group of experimenters? In any event, the track record of animal cloning, even at a bodily level, has been beset by difficulties, with thousands of deformed foetuses being discarded on the way to producing 'Dolly the sheep'.

2

The return:
biblical and historical background

The concept of the 'return' of a soul, or individual essence, to a new incarnation is not new. It is described or, at the very least, hinted at in the Bible. For example, when the disciples, after the death of John the Baptist, asked Jesus about him, Jesus told them that John had been a reincarnation of Elijah (Mark 9.11, Matthew 16.13, 17.12, Luke 9.18) – Elias in some translations – as set out and explored more fully in a later chapter.

It is also implicit in at least one parable, for it is notable that Jesus is not recorded as having rebuked those disciples who suggested that the suffering of the man born blind was the result of him having sinned in a previous life, or indeed that his affliction was the result of his parents having sinned (John 9.2).

The concept of reincarnation was established as a legitimate topic of speculation or belief in Jewish circles, especially amongst important and influential groups such as the Essenes. [64] The Essenes were avowedly separatist, whose main settlement, it is now generally thought, was located near the western shores of the Dead Sea, at Qumran, just a day or two's walk to the east of Jerusalem. And it has been suggested that the 'Damascus' to which Saul of Tarsus, later to become known as St Paul, the Apostle to the Gentiles, was heading, when struck by the blinding light that transformed his life and caused him to become a supporter of Jesus, was a code name for Qumran. [51] Hugh Schonfield in his book *The Passover Plot* wrote that Jesus could only have made his prophetic forecasts about those who would act against him, by interpreting the Scriptures in the way the Essenes did.

It is likely, though not currently accepted as certain, that the Essenes were the community associated with the Dead Sea Scrolls. This group rejected the sacrifices and priesthood of the officially recognised Jewish Temple at Jerusalem. In certain respects, the Essenes resembled the early Christian Church movement. They practised property sharing, and distributed money to those who needed it. Their lifestyle was frugal, and 'any member who had two coats, gave one away to his needy brother and wore his remaining coat until it was threadbare'. They devoted a lot of attention to the inner meaning of Scripture, and made predictions of the future which, as Schonfield indicates, was a pattern followed by Jesus in the manner adopted by this ascetic group. Indeed, Greek documents and sources liken the Essenes to ascetics who followed the style of Pythagorus. [10]

Even now, the Essenes may be making their influence felt, for it seems that some Vatican theologians are planning to work on a new translation of the Bible, which will incorporate a number of the variant texts found in the Dead Sea Scrolls, and the leader of this project is the historian Etienne Nodet, author of *The Origins of Christianity*. [4] Furthermore, reincarnation was taught by the Essenes, according to the Revd Leslie D. Weatherhead. [64] And even Pharisees and Sadducees differed as to their respective views of what happened after death (Acts 23.6–8).

The Pharisees were the religious grouping or party that were most anxious to preserve the traditional and distinctively religious character of Jewish life in defiance of Hellenistic – Greek – influences and Roman domination. Pharisees were very strict in their observance of the Law of Moses as well as the scribal tradition of interpretation of that Law. However, even within the Pharisaic tradition there were doctrinal conservatives and liberals.

The Sadducees, the other main group of Jewish religious leaders, tended to be drawn from the main aristocratic Jewish families, and held only to the Law of Moses, and did not feel themselves bound by scribal tradition. More importantly, in terms of belief about the afterlife, they rejected a belief in the resurrection of the dead, as St Paul was aware (Acts 23.6–8, as mentioned above). The Sadducees rejected such a belief in the resurrection on the grounds that it was 'a doctrine only found in writings like the book of Daniel, composed long after the time of Moses and so, in their view, lacked authority.' [10]

Christian groups, evolving as they did from Jewish ones, continued, not surprisingly, to debate and discuss this issue amongst themselves.

9

However, in later historical terms, sympathy towards belief in pre-existence and reincarnation received setbacks not only in AD 325, when Constantine imposed uniformity of belief on the newly Christianised Roman Empire but, arguably, more importantly a greater setback occurred in the year 553 when, under very dubious circumstances, the Emperor Justinian insisted that 'belief in the pre-existence of souls be declared anathema' at the influential, though arguably not 'official', Council of Constantinople, which effectively reinforced a decision made ten years earlier, at a local synod. The views and protests of the Popes of this era were, effectively, ignored. The background to this is explored more extensively in chapter 5. Perhaps the final remnants of belief in reincarnation at an organisational level received their next main and almost terminal setbacks around the thirteenth century, and this too is explored further in the next chapter. However, truth is never absolutely lost, however much officialdom at certain points of history may consider it to be unacceptable or inconvenient. This is and was as true in the Early Church as it is now, or indeed was at the time of Copernicus, Galileo, and Giordano Bruno.

Certainly sympathy towards the idea of the pre-existence of souls was not anathema to Church Fathers such as Origen, whose reputation is, at last, in the process of being rehabilitated by the work of some recently published academic authors whose books have reassessed his worth and influence.

The concept of pre-existence has also been written about in sympathetic terms in more recent times by churchmen such as The Revd Tom Strong, who gave the Canon Shepherd Memorial Lecture on the subject at the Old Palace, Worcester, in 1980. The Revd Leslie D. Weatherhead, one of the three best-known Methodists of the twentieth century in Britain, also wrote with an open mind, indeed sympathetically, about the concept of reincarnation. He said that those who supported the idea of rebirth in a reincarnational sense, included Joseph Glanvill, Chaplain to King Charles II, and Archbishop Passavalli (1820–1877), and that even St Augustine speculated about the topic in *The Confessions Book I.* [64]

In more modern times the *Catholic Encyclopaedia* records 'There is no barrier to belief in reincarnation for Catholic Christians'. [1] Such a view helps to explain why opinion-poll evidence concerning this subject in respect of Catholics indicates higher levels of support than is the case for other denominations. And there is one offshoot from the Church of Rome that probably has levels of support for the subject that are higher still, namely the Liberal Catholic Church. As their name implies, they tend to take a much more liberal view towards the matter, though such views tend to be expressed by individual priests rather than corporately.

Perhaps this open-minded approach is appropriate for what some may regard as a rather scientific topic – though in this case involving what might be called 'spiritual science' – just as the question of whether the Earth went around the Sun, or vice versa, raised scientific and theological questions for Galileo, Copernicus, and the Catholic Church in the Middle Ages. After all, if reincarnation does take place – and not just for prophets – presumably it does so even if we don't believe in it at the moment or cannot, at present, prove that it happens.

Even Pope John Paul II seemed to be, at least at some level, aware of the possibility of saints or Church leaders of the past reappearing in today's world, according to one newspaper when it reported that Gerard Depardieu had been granted a Papal audience. According to the French actor, as soon as he entered the room, the Pope exclaimed, with astonishment, that Depardieu looked exactly like St Augustine. It seemed to have been an entirely spontaneous and unpremeditated comment. The reference here is to St Augustine of Hippo, born in this Roman enclave of North Africa in the year AD 354, and not to the later Augustine who led a Catholic mission to Kent, England, at the end of the sixth century, following Pope Gregory's initiative in proposing this course of action. The report concluded by saying that Pope John Paul II had subsequently asked the actor, a Roman Catholic, to publicise Christian teachings by making a worldwide tour impersonating St Augustine, based on *The Confessions*, the Church Father's autobiographical writing, written in the fifth century.[5] Will Depardieu be permitted to include Augustine's speculations about pre-existence or reincarnation? It may even be, if the project is to continue following the death of John Paul II, that it is more likely under his successor, Pope Benedict XVI. For, as Cardinal Ratzinger, the subject of his first dissertation was St Augustine of Hippo.

Going back further in time, the fact that reincarnation was a common belief in Jewish circles 2000 years ago, is referred to by the Jewish historian Josephus, who wrote in *De Bello Judaico*: 'They say that all souls are incorruptible, but that the souls of good men are only removed into other bodies.'

So what then of the 'good men' (and women) who died in and around the World Trade Centre Building on September the 11th, 2001; and on July the 7th, 2005, in London? Will they, like others who die suddenly by war or accident for example, also have the opportunity of being 'removed into other bodies' at some future date? Indeed, would historical figures such as Josephus, or Augustine, or even the Emperor Justinian have returned, and if so, in what form? What are the characteristics that might distinguish them and that we might look out for?

Perhaps the matters to look out for are hinted at in Psalm 126 verse 6, as set out and further explored in chapter 8, with its reference to returning again with 'sheaves' which might, if indeed it is a reference to reincarnation, be another way of saying, 'Ye shall know them by their fruits' (Matt 7.16). These quotations indicate a form of divine justice, in that those who do good, may benefit from their beneficial actions, and not only in 'the afterlife', but in a future physical one, should there be one in their case. In such instances, might not justice be served by a future life to compensate for an unexpectedly truncated recent incarnation, as a consequence of the Twin Towers disaster in New York, for example?

For, as the one-time Poet Laureate, John Masefield, wrote:

> I hold that when a person dies,
> His soul returns again to earth;
> Arrayed in some new flesh-disguise,
> Another mother gives him birth.
> With sturdier limbs, and brighter brain,
> The old soul takes the road again. [64]

According to the *Dictionary of National Biography*, Masefield wrote not just poetry but also religious drama in which Christian teaching was taken seriously with plays such as *Good Friday*, *The Trial of Jesus*, and *The Coming of Christ*. These were undertaken by Masefield following his studies at Christ Church, Oxford, where he obtained a degree in Church History at the end of the nineteenth century. Though not an established theologian, he clearly had acquired a reasonably extensive knowledge of theology and ecclesiastical matters, and the comments on the soul's purpose as expressed in the quoted poem no doubt well described his view of a spiritual reality.

Many religious writers describe 'the immortality of the soul', and it is not entirely unreasonable to suppose that what exists after the death of the physical body, already existed before birth. If this point is accepted, then there is some logic to the argument for reincarnation. If this was a reality, then it would provide an opportunity for people such as Hitler and Nero to redeem any harm caused to others, by their actions in subsequent lives.

Then there is the point that well-known characters in history who lived good and honest lives, such as John the Baptist, might therefore be all the more likely to be the subject of prophetic forecast, especially if they had previously been prophets. Indeed, the return of the Baptist was described by Malachi in the Old (i.e. Jewish) Testament, when it was written: 'Behold, I will send you Elijah the Prophet before the coming of the great and dreadful day of the Lord' (Malachi 4.5).

King Solomon was also described as a good person, with the writer of the Book of Wisdom recording a description of him in this way: 'Being good, I came into a body undefiled' (8.20). Is the writer – perhaps Solomon himself – not here stating that Solomon's pre-existent soul was rewarded for being morally upright by being given a healthy body? [4]

In Romans 9.13, in the New Testament, Paul speaks about the Old Testament story of Rebecca's as yet unborn children, of whom the Lord said in Malachi 1.2–3 that he 'loved Jacob' and 'hated Esau'. As Paul goes on to say in Romans 14.9: 'Is there unrighteousness with God?' How could this pre-birth love and hatred be explained, other than by actions in their previous existences?

The traumatic events that took place on September the 11th, 2001 raise questions in the most public way – though there are of course many other examples – of what the New Testament calls 'sowing and reaping', as referred to in Galatians 6.7. The skills that have been developed and the good that has been achieved by the people who died, in such a high-profile way that day, may be attributes which stay with their soul or 'essence' if indeed they are reincarnated.

'Judgement' at the end of a person's life – whether or not the death is premature – is referred to in the New Testament's Epistle to the Hebrews. The New English Bible's translation 'after death comes judgement' (Hebrews 9.27) would seem to be not, as many people think, a reference to the Last Judgement at the end of the world, but to an immediate review or 'judgement' of the earthly life that has just been ended; a judgement not in terms of theological dogma, as in 'Can you recite the Apostles Creed without doubts or hesitation creeping in?' or even 'How often did you attend a place of worship last August?', but rather it might be 'How often did you help others?'. This question would be in line with the exhortation, even admonishment, contained in the Book of James (1.22) that says: 'But be ye doers of the word, and not hearers only.' Or the question asked might simply be: 'What good did you do?'

Such a 'judgement', or rather, assessment, might help the individual concerned to decide, in due course, if, or when, or under what circumstances his or her next incarnation should take place. After all, it would hardly seem to be fair if a life was brought to a premature end without that person being given a chance to complete whatever it was that was important to their soul purpose or 'mission' in life.

As to the phrase 'It is appointed unto men once to die' mentioned in Hebrews 9.27, a quotation that is often referred to by those who argue that the concept of reincarnation is 'unbiblical', an explanation might be that the author of Hebrews was not able consciously to remember anything about former incarnations, as was the case with John the Baptist when he denied that he had ever been Elijah (John 1.21). [4] This point is also made by one of the earliest of the Church Fathers, Justin Martyr (*circa* 100–165), who founded the first Christian school in Rome and was said to have been scourged and martyred there. In his *Dialogue with Trypho*, Justin speaks of the soul inhabiting more than once a human body, but that it cannot remember previous experiences.

If we have lived before, it has been argued, then what could be more likely than that a new body means that we forget the memories associated with the old one. [64] And a more scientific explanation may be that changes in hormone levels during childbirth produce memory loss. [56]

But if reincarnation is a reality for some, or many, what if a number of the people in, say, the aircraft that crashed into the World Trade Towers, or which might have crashed into the White House, had completed their last incarnational experience? If they had no need for more life experiences, might a future incarnation be unnecessary?

That such a possibility exists, thus reinforcing – at least to some extent – current orthodox theology, is hinted at by the quotation in the Book of Revelation that reads, 'Him that overcometh will I make a pillar in the temple of my God, and he shall go no more out' (3.12). To what might 'he … go no more out'? To a further incarnation?

Some of these biblical quotations that may refer to pre-existence or reincarnation will be considered in more detail in a later chapter; as will the views of some Christians, and those who were brought up as Christians, who have been sympathetic to the idea in more recent times.

3

The Early Church Fathers;
Francis of Assisi and Thomas Aquinas;
the Cathars

Would the aerial bombing in Afghanistan and Iraq, as well as the violence elsewhere around the world linked to the events of September the 11th, 2001, have occurred if we had realised, our political leaders included, that many of the Church Fathers had taught the doctrine and reality of rebirth? For thoughts about the practical repercussions of such a teaching as applied to the religions of 'the West' – including the Middle East – and the governments whose actions have been based on such teachings, might have helped to deter them from authorising acts of violence that inevitably have a particular spiritual consequence, that of reincarnation which, if true, affects all those involved.

The early teachings of Islam, after all, developed at least partly in response to the perceived reality of the teachings and actions of the Christians of that time, which in turn were a development of Judaism.

In the century before Islam came into being, those who had supported teachings about pre-existence and reincarnation had suffered, especially, during the persecutions of the middle part of the sixth century, with the closing down of the Platonic school in Athens, and the pronouncements against Origen and his teachings, by the Eastern Church. As a result, some of the persecuted sects turned for sanctuary to the Arab world. It was in this way that the Founder of Islam, Mahommed, 'learned of reincarnation from the Monks of a Nestorian Monastery at Busra. The Muslim holy book, the Koran, says explicitly: 'God generates beings and sends them back over and over again until they return to Him.' [32]

Busra, which may also have been known as Bustra or Bostra, would appear to be located not all that far from some of the places involved in the reincarnation story and mentioned in the New Testament, being south south-east of present-day Damascus, east south-east of the Sea of Galilee, around which Jesus and his disciples taught, and north north-east of Qumran. It is within about 125 miles of most of these locations, and as little as half this distance from some of them. Now if Mohammed learned of reincarnation from the monks of a Christian monastery at around the turn of the seventh century, this seems to show that the concept was still being spoken of at that time with, presumably, some seriousness by a Christian community in the Middle East. As part of such thinking, perhaps the community may have referred to the quotation in the Book of Revelation (3.12) which reads: 'Him that overcometh will I make a pillar in the temple of my God, and he shall go no more out', which seems not so dissimilar to the quotation mentioned in the Koran and set out above. Islamic perspectives are considered in more detail in chaper 6.

So what then did the Early Church teach about matters linked to the subject of reincarnation? Certainly the concept of 'pre-existence', in other words a previous incarnation, was held by leading members of the Church in Egypt, and especially in Alexandria. For example, St Clement, the early third-century Bishop of Alexandria, said: 'But we were before the foundation of the world, we who, because we were destined to be in Him, were begotten beforehand by God' (*Protrepticus*, translated by G.W. Butterworth, chapter 1). [4]

This Egyptian connection assumes particular importance because Jesus and the Holy Family spent some time in Egypt after fleeing Herod, as described in Matthew 2:

13 And when they were departed, behold, the angel of the Lord appeareth to Joseph in a dream, saying, Arise, and take the young child and his mother, and flee into Egypt, and be thou there until I bring thee word: for Herod will seek the young child to destroy him.

14 When he arose, he took the young child and his mother by night, and departed into Egypt:

15 And was there until the death of Herod: that it might be fulfilled which was spoken of the Lord by the prophet, saying Out of Egypt have I called my son.

Some commentators, including those who have received information via hypnosis, have recognised the similarities between the views and circumstances of Jesus, his parents, and his siblings, and the Essenes, who did believe in reincarnation. [36] It is very possible that this group had a centre in Egypt in which Jesus might have found sanctuary.

Egypt too was where one of the most important early Christian thinkers was based, who in many ways continued the work of Clement of Alexandria. Origen, born in the year 185, was the principal proponent of the concept of the pre-existence of the soul, and wrote:

> Is it not in conformity with reason that every soul ... is introduced into a body ... according to its deserts and former actions? The cause of each man's activities goes back into the past. Every soul comes into this world strengthened by the victories or weakened by the defeats of its previous life. The providence of God which governs the Universe with justice, also rules immortal souls with the merits and motives of each individual. [4]

This question of divine justice might perhaps also be applied to the circumstances of those who died amid the traumatic events of September the 11th, 2001, in New York. What were their 'merits' in this context? Could it be, based on this principle of divine justice, that if they had been pre-occupied mainly by materialistic matters, they might be given an opportunity of reincarnating again, but in less propitious circumstances than those whose lives had been predominantly selfless? Perhaps, in some cases – though certainly not all – this could relate to the theme being referred to in the prophesy mentioned in Ecclesiasticus, one of the books of the Apocrypha – though considered to be canonical by Roman Catholics – which says:

> Woe be unto you, ungodly men, which have foreseen the law of the most high God: for if ye increase, it shall be to your destruction; and if ye be born, ye shall be born to a curse; and if ye die, a curse shall be your portion (41.8–9).

Could the 'increase' referred to relate to the success in acquiring material wealth which enabled some of the victims to be at such a commercially prestigious address? Might the 'curse' relate to the unexpected disaster that caused them to die in such tragic circumstances? If Origen and Clement were right, then perhaps actions taken by the individuals

18

involved in some previous existence might have played some part in the process of cause and effect.

Origen had replaced Clement as Head of the Catachetical school at the age of eighteen. Had he merited this early advancement because of some merit obtained as the result of his efforts in a former life? Jerome, who produced a Latin translation of the Bible, considered Origen to be the greatest teacher of the Church after the Apostles. [4] And Origen is described by *The Catholic Encyclopaedia* as 'a man of virtue and genius, with a prodigious capacity for work.' The Western Church continued to read Origen and to appreciate him as exegete and spiritual director until around the end of the twelfth and the beginning of the thirteenth century, when the rise of Aristotelianism caused his influence to recede.

This latter period in history turns out to be crucial in terms of Church sympathy for the concept of pre-existence, and also for reincarnation, and it involves several individuals and groups, including people who had lived a millennium and a half earlier, whose teachings continued to be influential; Plato, Aristotle, Aquinas, the Dominicans, the Franciscans, and the Cathars, as well as Origen, amongst others.

The increased influence of the teachings of Aristotle, rather than those of Plato seems to have come about partly, if not mainly, because of Thomas Aquinas who followed, much more than hitherto had been the case with Church people, Aristotle who, unlike his tutor, Plato, was not sympathetic to the idea of predestination or reincarnation. Furthermore, Aquinas first started his theological training with the Dominicans at around the same time that the Cathars, rival Christians who *did* accept reincarnation as a reality, were being destroyed and burnt by the Crusaders in the last Cathar stronghold of Montsegur, in the year 1244.

The Dominicans were among the religious groups who were opposing the Cathars and therefore it would have been surprising if Aquinas had not accepted the Dominican views about the Cathars. Being of lively mind, and in sympathy with the views of his religious order, Aquinas looked for ways of opposing the Cathar beliefs, including their acceptance of reincarnation. The views of Aristotle would have helped him to do that, but those of Plato – and Origen, and those who followed Origen's school of thought – would not. Ostensibly, Aquinas was developing his ideas with a view to finding a middle way between the thoughts of Plato, and those of Aristotle; but in practice, they veered

19

towards Aristotle and, inevitably, downplayed the importance of Plato's teachings.

Aquinas, using the then recently translated works of Aristotle, put the emphasis on reason, rather than revelation, and this was found to be effective in countering the views of the Cathars and other groups, and thus the rise of Aristotelianism came about. The translations of Aristotle's works had been undertaken by Muslim writers, whose work had been brought back to France and other countries by earlier crusaders. Had they put the emphasis on translating, or re-translating, Plato's works instead, religious worldviews among the monotheistic religions might have developed in a very different way.

Indeed the views and thoughts of Aristotle, born in 384 BC, might not have had much religious influence in the West at all, had it not been for Aquinas, for the teachings of Aristotle had previously been suppressed by the Church, though the Muslim philosopher Averros, who died in the year 1178, had written the fullest commentary on Aristotle. This was over forty years before the birth of Aquinas who, much to the dismay of his family, decided to join the then fairly newly formed Dominicans, rather than the more established Benedictines. [53] The Dominicans though, had been founded with the specific intention of combating Catharism. [25] Aquinas then set about establishing what the true teachings of Aristotle were, and used Aristotle's methods to examine the Christian faith with a view to strengthening arguments that were based on reason. [53]

Aquinas had gone to study in Naples, rather than Paris, and this may well have influenced his research, because Paris was more sympathetic to the ideas of Plato. There is a certain historical irony, even poignancy in the fact that Aquinas chose the monastic order, and the historical teaching influence – Aristotelianism – *and* the particular teaching centre that most emphasised the views opposed to the idea of pre-existence of the soul and reincarnation. Aquinas wrote extensively and energetically and his life's work was contained in his *Summa Theologica*, that moved towards an explanation of belief and Christianity, a really quite massive piece of writing which, even in condensed form, can be found in theological bookshops today as one of the largest and heaviest books on the shelf. However, a further irony is that this work, which emphasised reason rather than revelation, remained unfinished. The reason for this seems to be that Aquinas had a revelation towards the end of his life which made him realise how little of the truth he knew, and so he ceased writing. Aquinas was made a saint, despite the indications in reference books that this was done on fairly slight evidence in terms of miracles, because of the influence of his writing, yet by the end of his life he had no wish to continue his summary of his life's writing.

Aquinas had joined the Dominicans when he was at the formative age of nineteen, just twenty-eight years after they were founded by Dominic. This was a crucial, indeed formative period for changing religious attitudes, for St Anthony of Padua was just twenty-one years of age when the Dominican Order was founded, so this too must have been a formative and impressionable age for this successor to St Francis as the leader of the Franciscans. And it was the Dominicans, supported by the Franciscans, who tackled and combatted the Cathars including their belief in reincarnation.

If the platonic worldview was undermined by Aquinas, then this was more or less what had happened some seven hundred years earlier when Origen's support for the platonic acceptance of the pre-existence of the soul was challenged by the Byzantine Emperor Justinian who, in his AD 543 *Anathemas* declaration concerning Origen, based his material on a dossier sent to a British monk who had criticised the doctrine of original sin, 'by the anti-Origenists, on various issues, most of which do not relate to pre-existence.'

Origen is generally regarded as being more important and influential in respect of this subject than Aquinas, but there is also the important question as to whether we now have a fair and accurate knowledge of what it was that Origen actually thought. After all this time, are we doing him and his views justice? Many of the opinions attributed to him may have just been those of others from the school which he led, rather as some of the letters of St Paul formerly attributed to him have since been attributed to others. In the case of Origen, most of what appears in his disputed discourses only remain to us today because they were quoted in the arguments of his opponents. And much of that, in turn, was first 'smoothed' by his translator, Rufinus, who did not want to offend the Church authorities. [18]

Jerome, whose translation of the Bible, the Vulgate, was adopted officially by the Catholic Church, described Origen as an 'immortal genius' with 'incomparable eloquence and knowledge'. And Adolf Harnack, the

German theologian, said that 'of all the theologians of the ancient Church, with the possible exception of Augustine, Origen is the most distinguished.' [4]

Chronologically, the next and most important theologian to comment on the subject, some two centuries later, was the indeed extremely influential St Augustine, the early fifth-century Bishop of Hippo, in north Africa, who said:

> The message of Plato … now shines forth mainly in Plotinus, a Platonist so like his master that one would think they lived together, or rather – since so long a period of time separates them – that Plato is born again in Plotinus.

Now Plotinus had died less than ninety years before Augustine was born, so his writings and teachings would have taken place relatively recently so far as Augustine was concerned.

There may be a sort of elliptical symmetry of coincidence that could link some of the major figures in Church history who have shown sympathy towards the doctrine of rebirth, or reincarnation; locational links too. For example, St Augustine, a Church Father, who at one time in his life asked himself rhetorically whether he had lived before. For Augustine to ask this question rhetorically, rather than stating it as opinion or fact, was not only intellectually honest, in the absence of certain knowledge, but also diplomatically astute. After all, to assert that one believed in reincarnation at that time in Church history might not have been politically or rather ecclesiastically advisable, given the attitude taken towards those who questioned the majority view from the time of the Emperor Constantine and the Council of Nicea onwards.

Now Augustine knew Pelagius – who was born around AD 370 – whose life and activities showed perhaps the first sign of the 'intellectual activity' of the Celtic Church, and spoke of him with great respect. [46] At least he did so in the earlier part of his life. Mercator said that Pelagius – whose native name was Morgan, thus indicating a Welsh connection – had borrowed his distinctive doctrines which emphasised the importance of the existence of free will, from Rufinus, the Syrian, which, though they didn't mention reincarnation, would nevertheless be compatible with an understanding or acceptance of the doctrine. Syria had, it might be said, a connection with the doctrine of reincarnation via the Druze of Syria,

22

who accepted the doctrine, and Jerome said that Rufinus was a pupil of Theodore of Mopsuestia and a student of Origen, the other main Church Father, apart from St Augustine, who had indicated a degree of sympathy for the doctrine of rebirth. [46]

So, somewhat convoluted though it may sound, Origen seems to have been what might be described as the intellectual grandfather of Pelagius, who was the acquaintance of Augustine, who also had written about the subject, albeit more speculatively.

Augustine also said in his *Confessions*,

> Did my infancy succeed another age of mine that dies before it? Was it that which I spent within my Mother's womb? ... And what before that life again ... was I anywhere or in any body? [27]

Thus someone who many regard as the greatest of the Fathers of the Church wonders whether Plotinus, who taught reincarnation, was himself a reincarnation of Plato, who also taught it.

These thoughts and speculations by Augustine sound very much like the message conveyed in Wordsworth's 'Ode to Immortality':

> Our birth is but a sleep and a forgetting
> The Soul that rises with us, our life's star,
> Hath had elsewhere its setting,
> And cometh from afar.
> Not in entire forgetfulness
> And not in utter nakedness
> But trailing clouds of glory do we come
> From God who is our home.

King Charles II's Chaplain, Joseph Glanvill seemed to be at ease with this theory, or indeed reality, when he wrote:

> Every soul brings a kind of sense with it into the world, whereby it tastes and relishes what is suitable to its peculiar temper. What can we conclude but that the soul itself is the immediate subject of all this variety and that it came prejudiced and prepossessed into this body with some implicit notions that it had learnt in another?

and that pre-existence was 'the constant opinion of the Jews, and therefore accepted by Christ and his Apostles' (*Lux Orientalis*, 1662). [27]

23

Glanvill quoted the story of Jesus healing the blind man, as described in John 9, as proving the acceptance of the concept and reality of pre-existence, when Jesus answered, in response to the question: 'Master, who did sin, this man, or his parents, that he was born blind?' by saying: 'Neither hath this man sinned, nor his parents.' The question asked, proved the presumption, he said. Such a view expressed by the influential Joseph Glanvill, that Christ and his Apostles accepted pre-existence, is a most important point, and supports the idea that pre-existence of the soul may be seen to be an acceptable part of Christian thinking, if not that of Judaism too. And the Pharisees *presumed* existing sinfulness in verse 34, 'Thou wast born in sins'. Ganvill's views are again reviewed in chapter 9.

Acceptance of the idea of pre-existence and even reincarnation in the western world extended beyond Judaism. For example Plato, in his *Phaedo*, indicated that, with certain exceptions, 'many revolutions of ages' ensue between lives. Virgil makes a similar claim. [27] Now if it is true that there are very long periods, on average, between incarnations, then this would help to counter the argument that reincarnation cannot be a reality because the numbers living on the Earth have increased enormously over, say, the last two thousand years. If there are vastly greater numbers of souls out of incarnation, or living in other parts of the solar system, then this increase in numbers might be of comparatively little consequence in the overall scheme of things.

Such matters, no doubt, were discussed even as late as the early-thirteenth century between those who were sympathetic towards such ideas, even within the Church and the new monastic movements, thus reflecting the comments made by the Desert Fathers and theologians of, for example, the fifth century.

Comments that St Augustine had been at one time sympathetic to the Platonic traditions – which were known to support the idea of rebirth, or reincarnation – are echoed some seven hundred years later, at the time of St Francis, in the late twelfth century. Steven Rosen writes of a link between the platonic traditions and the early Franciscan ones which, he says, were more sympathetic to a philosophy that includes reincarnation than the Aristotelian view; Aristotle being Plato's primary disciple, who did not share his teacher's enthusiasm for the idea, [56] as previously said.

St Francis of Assisi, however, was said to have accepted the concept of reincarnation [64], and he is especially important if this is true, for he has been an enormously influential and important saint, as previously mentioned, as he was named as the Patron Saint of Ecology by Pope John Paul II. If it is indeed correct that he believed in reincarnation, what would he have said, were he to be alive today, about the implications involved in the environmental damage and deaths caused in New York on September the 11th, 2001 and subsequently in Afghanistan and Iraq in particular? These ecological consequences are further described and explored in chapter 10. St Francis' influence has of course played an important part in the development of monastic communities, which have usually taken environmental issues seriously, as well as having a philosophical influence on the whole environment movement.

'But why', it might be asked, 'if Francis of Assisi accepted the concept of reincarnation, does not the Franciscan movement of today generally accept it?' The answer may lie with the man who succeeded St Francis.

Francis of Assisi died in 1226, but after the year 1227, the Franciscans were governed by someone called Anthony, originally from Lisbon, in Portugal, but later from Padua, where he had taught theology. He, in turn, was canonised not long afterwards, and within a year of his death in 1231, at the early age of thirty-six, as St Anthony. Like St Francis, he was a great lover of animals as well as of flowers, of trees, and fish, and he preached vigorously both in Lombardy and in the South of France, where Anthony had a reputation for being ultra orthodox in his theology.

Perhaps this conservative theological thinking may be linked to his experience of teaching in a more formal ecclesiastical setting, or perhaps the cause of it, and may explain why any sympathy towards the Cathars and their acceptance of the doctrine of, or reality of, reincarnation, held by St Francis and perhaps the Franciscans during the time of their founder, could have been dissipated or even reversed during the time that St Anthony held sway. And also subsequently, for the time of his demise coincided with the final campaign to eliminate the Cathars, whose final defeat in France took place at their stronghold of Montsegur, just thirteen years later.

The Cathars

The era in which St Francis lived was famous for another hugely influential movement of that time, the Cathars. They had their main strongholds of support in south-west and southern France, not much more than five hundred miles, as the crow flies, from where St Francis lived in Italy, though some Cathar teachers 'travelled freely through northern Italy, and even further afield'. [16] In a book written by a medical doctor, and very much from the Cathar standpoint, and which to a large extent relies on revelations from one of his patients, he describes the Cathars in ways that indicate that they had a number of patterns of existence that were similar to those of St Francis, even though he may not have overtly espoused support for them, which would have been ecclesiastically and 'politically' difficult at the time. The Cathar priests are described as having 'above all to be spiritually pure, combining this with compassion and understanding.' [21]

St Bernard, who took part in a preaching mission to the heart of the Cathar-influenced area of present day France in the year 1147, said of the Cathars: 'examine their mode of life; you will find nothing more irreproachable.' St Bernard became Abbot of Clairvaux, which became a chief centre of the Cistercian Order, whose lifestyle was designed to emphasise austerity.

The general orthodox Catholic Church rule of that time was that no lay person was permitted to possess a copy of the Scriptures. However Cathar groups possessed a manuscript of some sort that seems to have had links with the Gospel period of the Early Church, or at least the Cathars believed that it did. Therefore the existence of this group and widespread support for them amongst much of the general populace in south western and southern France, and even north west Italy has therefore been regarded as being an early and quasi Protestantism, in the sense that the Cathars set and continued to set great store by the ability to be able to read for themselves the Gospel teachings. And because the Cathars had a particular affinity or link with what seems to have been a form of St John's Gospel, this too has an uncanny link with modern evangelical Protestantism, which also tends to emphasise the importance of passages from St John's Gospel. The crusade to extirpate the Cathars related, at least partially, to their claim to have original source material in the form of the Fourth Gospel, even an original manuscript of it. [3] Could this version of St John's Gospel have taught reincarnation, as another version, discussed in later chapters, did?

The manuscript carried by and referred to by the Cathars certainly emphasised the pure life. However, whatever the document was, for

Catharism, doctrine was secondary. 'What they stressed most of all, was life and example. For them, the true disciples of Christ were those who copied His life and the example of the way He lived, who reverenced His teaching, and who lived in obedience to it.' [3] One of the best known, if not *the* best known of the Cathar Bishops, Guilabert of Castres, at a crucial public debate in Palmiers, in the year 1207, said: 'I have given up everything the Gospel commands me to renounce; gold and silver I no longer carry in my purse. I am satisfied with each day's food and am not anxious whether tomorrow I shall have the where-withal to be clothed and fed.' He went on to tell his listeners that they beheld in him, as a Cathar representative, the beatitudes which Jesus Christ preached: 'You see me poor, meek, peaceable, pure in heart; you see me in tears, suffering hunger and thirst, persecution and the world's hatred for the sake of righteousness.' [3]

Now if their version of St John's Gospel also taught reincarnation as a means by which they understood the context of, and followed the teachings given by Jesus, would this have led the Cathars to become the peace-loving people that most of them or indeed almost all of them, seemed to be, and if so, could this have lessons for us in the world today, and especially in the trouble spots, and potential trouble spots of the world? After all, could the Cathars, scrupulous as they were in their lifestyle, and following what they understood to be the teachings of Jesus via their version of St John's Gospel, have taught of the reality of reincarnation, if they thought for one moment, that Jesus had not taught such a Universal Law?

But might there be another reason why St John's Gospel took such a hold in the imagination of the ordinary people of southern France, or rather what we now know as southern France, but which in earlier times was known as Gaul. Could St John's Gospel have been physically brought to Cathar-influenced areas? From another source, it has been said that St John was the first disciple who came to France, and that Cathars believed that St John brought Christianity 'to France just as Joseph of Arimathea did to Britain'. [65]

The crusade against the Cathars, some have said, was even more deter-mined and extreme than that undertaken against the Saracens, because the Cathars claimed unbroken apostolic succession since the time of the dispersion described in the New Testament and were thus seen as a threat

27

to the established teachings of that era from a Church perspective. [3] However, it may be that the secular authorities of the time, encouraged by the established ecclesiastical authorities took especially rigorous action partly because there was land and property to be gained whereby the territory of northern France could be extended to include the south, and because from a religious perspective, the threat of 'dualism' was felt to be especially acute, even though the Cathars based this approach on Scripture, and on 1 Corinthians 15 in particular.

But even if in these present times it is felt that the action taken to exterminate the Cathars would now be unacceptable – for who would now advocate the extermination of the Orthodox or all Protestants if their views were thought to be unacceptable? – it may be that the truths that the Cathars taught, and especially their lifestyle, and perhaps also reincarnation, especially if it can be shown to have been an authentic and original Christian teaching, should be rescued from the rubble of history. In any event, one person at least, did rescue at least some aspects of the way that Cathars lived and thought, and that was St Francis, who with his father, seems to have had a fair amount of sympathy for Catharism. [12] It certainly seems that Catharism came to the Languedoc in south west France in the eleventh century, via Italy, where Cathars were known as the *Paterini.* [3]

The major religious changes that took place in the Languedoc in the century or more that followed the invasion of England by William, Duke of Normandy, were indeed to a large extent the result of struggles over territory. During this time, much if not all of the south and south western parts of present day France were independent of the French Kings, and differed widely from the north in terms of manners and of language. It was the home of chivalry and of song, whose inhabitants were proud of their learning, and who regarded the less sophisticated and rougher north with a certain contempt. 'The peoples of Languedoc and Provence' themselves however 'protested against the riches and corruption of the clergy, and sought to bring back the Christian religion to the simplicity of the time of the Apostles.' [47]

From a religious point of view, they were sometimes if not usually called Albigensians, because the Diocese of Albi was regarded as the centre of their sphere of influence. Moreover, the Albigensians 'who were tolerant of all opinions, were friendly to the Jews' who, rather like the Cathars in the years that followed, had been persecuted by many, but who 'enjoyed freedom and consideration in the south of France'. There the Jews 'possessed land, held high office in the towns, and had synagogues and schools from which travelled doctors and philosophers, who spread abroad the learning they had gained' from 'the Arabs'. This tolerance towards the Jews, however, was regarded by those in the north of France as 'a scandal and an offence'. [47]

Could the presence of, and support for the Jews in southern France at that time, before the Crusade launched by Pope Innocent III, have a connection with the version of the Gospel of John that was said to have been brought to this area and which was so popular with the Albigensians, or Cathars? And did this version of the Gospel thus cause the Cathars to accept, at least for most people, the concept of reincarnation, as other versions of this Gospel may have done, as described in subsequent chapters?

The activities of the Cathars, and to a greater extent than is generally appreciated, their beliefs also, were not only shared by St Francis of Assisi, but, anticipated by about fifty years, others too. For in the latter part of the twelfth century a number of groups, including one known as the Waldensians, or Vaudois, were keen to follow and disseminate both biblical practice and teaching. They were led by Peter Valdo, a rich citizen of Lyon who, appalled by the spiritual ignorance of the local population, distributed all his goods to the poor and, with his disciples, went about preaching. He also arranged for the Gospels and some other parts of the Bible to be translated into the common language of the region. His teaching included obedience to the command not to swear an oath, or to kill, and he rejected the practice of granting indulgences, a view which echoed that of Martin Luther, many centuries later. [3]

The Waldensian initiative and the activities and beliefs of the Cathars with whom they were perhaps inevitably though somewhat erroneously linked, given their similar emphasis on the importance of Scripture, were in great contrast to those of the individuals who wielded authority in Rome, some fifty years later in the early thirteenth century, who instituted a ban on any lay person possessing a copy of the Scriptures. The only exception to this rule concerned the liturgy, though this had to be in Latin, rather than the language of most ordinary people. [3]

By contrast, the Cathars in particular had made a profound study of New Testament writings and encouraged their followers to study them too. Rather as Peter Valdo did, they translated the New Testament into the popular language, and quoted a number of particular texts in support of their views. Two verses from one of the apostolic letters seem to have been of especial interest to them, namely 1 Corinthians 15:

40 There are also celestial bodies, and bodies terrestrial: but the glory of the celestial is one, and the glory of the terrestrial is another.
44 It is sown a natural body; it is raised a spiritual body. There is a natural body, and there is a spiritual body.

A reference, perhaps, to the distinction made between the soul, and the physical body, which may be echoed in another verse popular with the Cathars: 2 Corinthians 5:

1 For we know that if our earthly house of this tabernacle were dissolved, we have a building of God, an house not made with hands, eternal in the heavens.

Perhaps a double meaning might also be being referred to in 1 Peter 3.19 '... he went and preached unto the spirits in prison' – another popular Cathar text – the 'he' in this case, referring to Christ, and the 'prison' referring, in addition to the more obvious literal meaning of 'jail', to the bodily 'prison' of the soul, in the view of the Cathars. [3]

There would also seem to be a reference to such a double meaning in a quotation from the Gospel that the Cathars liked so much: John17.16: 'They are not of the world, even as I am not of the world.' Again, the Cathars thought that this was a reference to the soul level, rather than a personality level which the Cathars believed would not reincarnate.

The view has been expressed that the Cathars wanted to return direct to the true Heaven world, and not to be reincarnated in any lower spheres of existence. By comparison, though, 'the Gnostics said that a reappearance on these lower spheres is a "recurrence", rather than a "re-incarnation".'[7] Perhaps this terminology means rather different things to different groups throughout history that have divergent world views.

Though they generally preferred the New Testament to the Old, nevertheless the Albigensians did have a liking for some Old Testament Books, 'notably the Prophets and the Psalms'. Of the latter, they liked quoting Psalm 142:

7 Bring my soul out of prison, that I may praise thy name: the righteous shall compass me about; for thou shalt deal bountifully with me

as another indication of the distinction between the soul, and the body representing the personality. The Cathars respected the Gospel of St John above the others because they regarded it as representing the most authentic teaching, at least in their version of the Gospel, and because they felt that St John was the one disciple who best understood what Jesus taught and represented. [3] Furthermore the earliest historical mention of Jesus, at the time of writing, is in a papyrus fragment from the Gospel of John, written in Greek in about AD 125.[8] And the Gospel of John was the most popular Gospel in southern France.

In the part of south-west France known as Gaul, the Count of Toulouse was effectively the ruler of this vast area when the Cathars' success amongst the populace was at its height, and he extended his sway and influence to the borders of Italy.

It may not be widely appreciated that the city of Toulouse was far wealthier and more heavily populated at the end of the twelfth century than Paris, or even London, or indeed any other city apart from Rome, at least in Europe. Catharism was mainly concentrated in the area between the Dordogne river and the border with what is now Spain.

At the end of the twelfth century, Raymond VI, Count of Toulouse, was a Cathar sympathiser, and in 1198, Pope Innocent III was enthroned in St Peter's, Rome, and he was the person who initiated missions to the areas influenced by the Cathars. The most successful of these missions, was one that led by example, compared with the quite money-based and extravagant lifestyle of the Catholic Church that had hitherto been evident in that area. This change of policy and tactic, was the result of advice given by the Spanish Bishop of Osma, who said: 'Go and teach after the example of the Divine Master, in humility, on foot, not with a sumptuous retinue, but penniless, like the Apostles.' The Pope at once approved of the new venture, which was led by the Bishop, accompanied only by his sub-prior, Dominic; and from this initiative grew the future Order of St Dominic. [3]

So, therefore, much of the monastic movement, subsequently, and certainly still today so environmentally aware and concerned with simple living, including Cistercians, Franciscans, and Dominicans, were inspired and preceded by, and in a certain sense 'led' by the Cathars, even though doctrinally they did not, in most respects, agree, but crucially, in terms of lifestyle, they came, ironically, to become rather similar. The Dominicans were, though, more successful in Italy than in France, and there, especially with the Franciscans, applied the Cathar methods of humility and poverty. The other main monastic tradition, the Benedictines, originating nearly seven hundred years earlier, also led a simple life. By 'coincidence', they too were founded at a time when the subjects of pre-existence and reincarnation were being debated and challenged, as will be described in a later chapter. There seems to be something of a correlation between the founding of monastic traditions, and wars and conflicts at a time of debate and reassessment of these subjects. And one Catholic priest wrote that St Basil was recorded as having said: 'The first thing to do is to interrupt the cycle of previous lives.' St Benedict had been much influenced by St Basil, whose own written guidelines for living were used and adapted by St Benedict in formulating his own rule. [41]

Bearing in mind the needs of the world, following the 'recent' war in Iraq, which will come to hold sway? The eagle, as a symbol of the United States, or the dove of peace, which most Church leaders now seem to identify with in this situation. The peaceable approach of the Cathars might be instructive here, for their symbol was also the dove of peace.

But to return to the example set by the Cathars, which may help to guide us as to the way in which we might live more peaceably today. The aspirant who wished to become a Cathar priest had to live 'a life of chastity, meditation, fasting, and good works', and 'they abstained from animal food'. The Cathars taught that reincarnation was a reality, though their goal, through their way of life, seems to have been that of achieving 'perfection', presumably with a view to escaping what they regarded as a potentially continuing cycle of reincarnation. The Cathars regarded themselves as Christians, and the view has been taken that in contemplating Catharism, 'one is returning to primitive Christianity'. [21] It is especially interesting in view of what is discussed in other chapters that their guiding Scripture was said to be John's Gospel, or a version of John's Gospel. In the Middle Ages, this group, or movement, is probably the best known amongst those with links to Christianity to have believed in reincarnation, though their activity was effectively ended when two hundred leading Cathars were burnt to death following the ending of the siege of their stronghold within the castle at Montsegur, near Toulouse in March 1244.

Reports of the events of this era, and in this locality have been recorded by the register of the Inquisition of that time. But, as in the

Bible, remarkable information can be provided by dreams and, in this case, checked against the historical facts recorded by the Church Authorities. [21] One such example in respect of the Cathar denouement at Montsegur, is described in great detail in Dr Guirdham's writings. His patient seemed able to recall the events of that time without reading about it in books. For example, she revealed, via dreams, that Cathar priests sometimes wore dark blue robes, a fact not known in recent times, until revealed in 1965, by Monsieur Jean Duvernoy, of Toulouse, in translating and editing the reports of the Inquisition. However Dr Guirdham's patient had had this information revealed to her, and recorded it in writing, as long ago as 1944. This might possibly be of little significance except that it reinforces the sometimes important subject of 'coincidence'. This modern revelation came exactly seven hundred years after the Cathar leaders suffered their harrowing end in the year 1244, surrounded by the attacking army of English soldiers on their way to the Crusades.

In the context of September the 11th, another important coincidence may involve the famous Muslim warrior, Saladin, defeated by the Crusaders who were proceeding towards Jaffa, on the Mediterranean coast. This all took place in the battle of Arsouf which was Saladin's first and only major defeat, after which the crusaders then continued on the way to their destination, arriving three days later. The first morning they spent in comparatively peaceful surroundings within the walls of the city, was on September the 11th. Saladin meanwhile, made his way to Ascalon, further along the coast, just south of Caesarea, to meet his friends and colleagues who commiserated with him. He arrived there on September the 11th, in the year 1191, [35] exactly eight hundred and ten years before the events of September the 11th, 2001, in New York.

Another coincidence recorded by Dr Guirdham, is that the main battle between the reincarnation-believing Cathars, or rather their militant supporters, and the Crusaders, took place on September the 11th in the year 1213. [22] In other words exactly 788 years to the day, before the destruction of the Twin Towers in New York. A most uncanny, even eerie coincidence. It was the battle of Muret, in which 'The combined forces of the Languedoc and the king of Aragon were defeated by Simon De Monfort' of Leicester, and his Crusaders. 'Muret was the real graveyard of the hopes of the Languedoc from the military and political point of view.' [22] And it may be something close to a potentially interesting coincidence that the most influential British politician with responsibility for responding to the aftermath of the events of September the 11th, 2001, was Tony Blair who, with his family, went to stay for his 2002 summer holiday, in the village of Le Vernet, France.[9] This area is less than twenty-five miles, as the crow flies, to the battle site of Muret, both of which are located to the south of Toulouse, in the Languedoc.

There is perhaps an uncanny poignancy to the Cathar prophesy:

Al Cap des set cens ans
verdegeo le laurel.

After seven hundred years
the laurel will be green again. [21]

Prophecies can, and do get fulfilled and perhaps this also anticipates a revival in the green, environmental movement after the second world war, which to some extent at least, was based on the example set by the monastic movements, which in turn were largely set by the 'green' Cathar movement that emphasised a lifestyle based on simple, ecological, and spiritual living.

4

Other comments from
Jewish and early Christian times

Would some of the violence and cycle of retribution in the Middle East, around Israel and Iraq, have been at least mitigated if the early Christians together with their successors, as well as the pre-cursors of the Christians, had accepted the concept of reincarnation? Or, if it was realised that many of them did so?

Jews in New Testament times, whether they were Essenes or Pharisees or Sadducees, were keen to find out whether Jesus was in fact the expected Messiah and saviour of the Jewish people, or indeed if he was a reincarnation of one of the Old Testament seers for, as Mark 8.27–28 says: 'Whom do men say that I am? And they answered, John the Baptist: but some say Elias; and others, one of the prophets.'

In John 1.21, John the Baptist is approached by priests and others from Jerusalem: 'And they asked him ... Art thou Elias? And he saith, I am not. Art thou that prophet? And he answered, No.' Thus it seems, from the questions asked of John and, later, of Jesus, that the Jews of this period were expecting the rebirth not only of Elias, otherwise known as Elijah, but perhaps other prophets too.

The importance of the reappearance, or reincarnation, of Elijah is therefore heavily emphasised in the Gospels. Some scholars, such as members of 'The Jesus Seminar' in the USA, seek to authenticate the genuineness of the reported teaching by the number of times a particular saying or parable is repeated in the four Gospels. In the case of the prophecy concerning the reappearance of Elijah foreshadowed in the Old Testament book of Malachi, the Hebrew prophet, in chapter 4 verse 5 writes: 'Behold, I will send you Elijah the prophet before the coming of the great and dreadful day of the Lord.'

Matthew refers to this prophecy on three occasions, and the remaining Gospels mention it seven times. Although some writers such as the second- and third-century Carthaginian theologian, Tertullian, argue that Elias did not die in the first place, but simply went up by a whirlwind into heaven, nevertheless Jesus says, without qualification, of John the Baptist: 'This is Elias, which was for to come' (Matthew 11.14). Therefore theologians and others who accept that Jesus was the expected Messiah would, as a matter of logic, have to believe in or accept rebirth – in Elijah's case at least – Elias and Elijah being one and the same person.

To return to New York – views of Hassidic Jews

Hassidism, an influential movement which had its beginnings with those who started their own 'pure' community at Qumran, by the Dead Sea, and whose activities seemed, elsewhere, to have undergone a revival in the eighteenth century among Polish Jews, has one of its most important centres of learning in Brooklyn, New York. According to the *Universal Jewish Encyclopaedia*, reincarnation is a universal belief in Hassidism. The Nazis destroyed many of its great centres of learning in World War II, but the strong New York connection remains. [28] The Hassidic play, *The Dybbuk*, written by S. Ansky, is described by this encyclopaedia as 'his masterpiece … taken from actual Hassidic life', and includes the following passage:

[If a man dies prematurely] what becomes of the life he has not lived …?

What becomes of his joys and sorrows, and all the thoughts he had no time to think, and all the things he hadn't time to do …?

No human life goes to waste.

If one of us dies before his time, his soul returns to earth to complete its span, to do the things left undone and experience the happiness and griefs he would have known …

It's not only the poor it pays to be careful with. You can't say for a certainty, who any man might have been in his last existence, nor what he is doing on earth … the human soul is drawn by pain and grief, as the child to its mother's breast, to the source of its being, the Exalted Throne above.

But it sometimes happens that a soul which has attained to the final state of purification suddenly [through pride?] becomes the prey of

36

evil forces which cause it to slip and fall. And the higher it has soared, the deeper it falls ...

[Such] vagrant souls which, finding neither rest nor harbour, pass into the bodies of the living, in the form of a Dybbuk, until they have obtained purity ...

The souls of the dead do return to earth, but not as disembodied spirits.

Some must pass through many forms before they achieve purification. [28]

The Hassidim came into the news more recently as the result of a newspaper report of an apocalyptic warning from a non-human source. It took place in New York, in the middle of March, 2003, just as Members of Parliament in Britain were preparing to vote on whether to join the USA for a war in Iraq; perhaps, in the circumstances, the date might be called 'the Ides of March', thus echoing the warning given to the Emperor Julius Caesar, that presaged disaster, for him at least, in the days of the Roman Empire. The event that affected the Hassidim in America's commercial capital involved what seemed to many of them to be a mystical cry of a prophetic nature, when a carp that was about to be killed, it was said, began to shout warnings concerning the near future. A few of the Hassidim Elders believed that this was, effectively, God's voice calling out. Other Elders among the Hassidim thought that the fish might have been, in effect, the voice of a recently deceased community Elder who was issuing the warnings of a divine nature. Zalman Rosen, who was one of the two witnesses to the event, and himself a Hassid, said that the words, which were spoken in Hebrew, meant that the time had now come to account for themselves, because the end was near at hand. The carp said that Rosen should himself pray and study the teachings of his religious faith. The other witness to the event was a committed Christian who, though he did not understand the words being spoken by the fish, did confirm that the carp had actually spoken. [10]

Though some may think that the story described in the newspaper report of this happening to be impossible, or at best, highly implausible, nevertheless it has strong echoes of the story in the Bible about Balaam's Ass, who was said to have spoken to Balaam in the Book of Numbers, chapter 22:

28 And the LORD opened the mouth of the ass, and she said unto Balaam,
    What have I done unto thee, that thou hast smitten me these three times?

Certainly the Bible indicates that such animal or non-human speech is
possible, and for those that believe in miracles, such a happening should
not therefore be beyond the bounds of possibility. At the very least, in the
circumstances of the second war in Iraq with all its attendant horrors that
have still not ended, despite the claim of 'victory', it does provide food
for thought.

The theme of reincarnation in the context of Jewish thought also came
to light during another warlike time, in England, when Rabbi Manasseh
Ben Israel (1604–1657), who was a theologian and statesman, asked
Oliver Cromwell to remove the legal prohibition of Jews from living in
England, which had existed for three hundred and fifty years since the
reign of Edward I. In his book *Nishmath Hayem* he wrote about the concept of the passing of the soul into another body as

> a firm and infallible dogma accepted by the whole assemblage of our
> church with one accord, so that there is none to be found who would
> dare to deny it. Indeed, there are a great number of sages in Israel who
> hold firm to this doctrine so that they made it a dogma with acclama-
> tion ... as the truth of it has been incontestably demonstrated by the
> Zohar, and all the books of the Kabalists. [28]

The reference to The Zohar is to a book which tradition ascribes to
Rabbi Simeon ben Jochai, as author. During the siege of Jerusalem in the
latter part of the first century AD, he escaped from the city and hid in a
cave for twelve years. After his death two disciples, Rabbi Eliezar and
Rabbi Abba, collected some of the manuscripts that he left, and compiled
them into a book. This was the original Zohar – The Book of Splendour.
In the year 1280, some six years after the death of Thomas Aquinas, the
Zohar reappeared, this time compiled and edited in Spain by Rabbi
Moses de Leon. The Zohar is in five sections, the last being entitled 'the
Book of the Revolutions of Souls', and includes the following description
of the process:

> All souls are subject to the trials of transmigration; and men do not
> know the designs of the Most High with regard to them; they know
> not how they are being at all times judged, both before coming into

this world, and when they leave it. They do not know how many transformations and mysterious trials they must undergo; how many souls and spirits come to this world without returning to the palace of the divine king.

The souls must re-enter the absolute substance whence they have emerged. But to accomplish this end, they must develop all the perfections, the germ of which is planted in them; and if they have not fulfilled this condition during one life, they must commence another, a third, and so forth, until they have acquired the condition which fits them for re-union with God. [28]

Not all Jews, it seems, accepted this concept as an integral part of Judaism, but some did, including a number of orthodox Rabbis. One well-known person from the first century AD, who spoke about reincarnation in a very matter-of-fact way, was the Jewish historian Flavius Josephus, in his highly regarded work *The Jewish War*. As a General in the campaign against the Roman Commander Vespasian, who had been sent by Nero to defeat the Jewish revolt, he had been one of the few survivors of a very gory siege. Addressing the Jewish soldiers who were about to commit suicide rather than be captured by the Romans, he said:

The bodies of all men are, indeed mortal, and are created out of corruptible matter; but the soul is ever immortal, and is a portion of the divinity that inhabits our bodies ... Do not you know, that those who depart out of this life according to the law of nature ... enjoy eternal fame: that their houses and their posterity are sure; that their souls are pure and obedient, and obtain a most holy place in heaven, from whence, in the revolution of ages, they are again sent into pure bodies; while the souls of those hands have acted madly against themselves are received by the darkest place in Hades? [28]

Josephus also describes how two of the three chief schools of Jewish thought, the Pharisees, and the Essenes believed, in varying degrees, that souls not only lived on, but could return in certain circumstances. The Pharisees 'say that all the souls are incorruptible, but the souls of good men only, are removed into other bodies, but the souls of bad men are subject to eternal punishment,' according to Josephus. With the Jews, it seems, 'eternal' did not mean everlasting, but simply a very long time.

39

In *The Antiquities of the Jews*, Josephus repeats that the Pharisees believe that the virtuous 'shall have power to revive and live again' on earth, 'on account of which doctrines they are able greatly to persuade the body of the people'. [27] This rather infers that such a view appealed to the majority of the population, rather than just a minority. It also raises the interesting question as to whether St Paul, who described himself as a Pharisee, and, what is more, the son of a Pharisee (Acts 23.6), accepted reincarnation for the virtuous. This matter is explored more fully in chapter 8.

There may well be similarities of worldview between Josephus and Saul of Tarsus who was the first to have responsibility for taking the Christian message to the non-Jewish world when he had an experience of the risen Christ. Certainly they were more or less contemporaries, and apart from his knowledge of the Pharisaic view of life after death, Josephus said of himself that he had the gift of prophecy, which he was able to make use of in his encounter with Vespasian, when forecasting that the latter would become Roman Emperor, which duly came about. And it has been said too that Josephus was a Pharisee. Certainly when Saul of Tarsus became St Paul, following his experience on the road to Damascus, he would have retained this knowledge of the Pharisaic worldview, and indeed did so, as Acts 23.6–9 makes clear. Hugh Montefiore took the view that Paul did not accept reincarnation. [42] However, others interpret this situation differently, as the next few paragraphs may serve to illustrate.

Prior to AD 70 and the destruction of the Temple in Jerusalem, the Pharisees 'considered it of paramount importance that one should die free of sin. With this in view, they instituted ways in which a condemned sinner could erase the sin from his soul, including confession, and the offer of one's life in payment for his sins.' Therefore, when Paul wrote that God allowed the death of Jesus to atone for the sins of all he, Paul, was in some ways saying what struck a chord with the Pharisees and the population at large – in other words, probably the majority – who sympathised with Pharisaic thinking and teaching. [20]

But there were two schools of Pharisaism – the conservative school of Shammai, and the liberal school of Hillel, and Paul had been brought up in the tradition of the latter. In her book *On Reincarnation: the Gospel according to Paul*, the author Marilyn Graham argues that Saul, before his conversion, therefore, was the sort of Pharisee who believed himself to have been condemned to rebirth, suffering, and death, but that Paul, the Christian, following his conversion, was the sort of Pharisee, or rather ex-Pharisee, who believed himself to be someone who now stood in hope of the end of that process. Thus Paul in his teaching, and in his more theological letters such as the Epistle to the Romans, combined his Pharisaic knowledge of the unwritten 'laws', including those quite possibly or even probably, of reincarnation, with the views of his Greek counterparts, thus being, as he puts it, 'all things to all men', as described in 1 Corinthians 9.22. [20]

The question of presumptions and assumptions concerning the worldview of Paul and other New Testament writers, has often caused problems for present day scholars. For example, the theologian James Dunn has expressed this in the following terms:

> Only when we can take for granted what Paul and his readers took for granted with regard to the law and its function, will we be able to hear the allusions he was making, and understand the arguments he was offering. [20]

The reference here to 'the law' is an interesting one because the 'law' took several forms, including legal, and – more importantly – divine 'law'. God's immutable law of justice might well be represented by the sort of Pharisaic worldview concerning reincarnation described by Marilyn Graham. Such an approach too, would make more sense of Ecclesiastes 2.12: '... for what can the man do who comes after the king? Only what he has already done.'

In other words, the best that Solomon, already a 'philosopher king', could hope for, would be to return, in a future incarnation, as a philosopher king, once again.

This would provide, if the presumed worldview involving reincarnation were to be accepted, a missing 'matrix' of the sort that would answer many of the difficult questions that scholars such as James Dunn, who analysed the Book of Romans, for example, have puzzled over. Paul, in his Letter to the Romans, and writing in a pre-AD 70 Pharisaic context, was anticipating objections from his Jewish and Roman and Pagan and Gentile audience – many if not most of whom may have accepted the existence of a 'Divine Law' of reincarnation.

41

5

The Council of Constantinople: a watershed; pre-existence; the fall from orthodoxy

Christianity finally came to be corralled into the ecclesiastical orthodoxy of the early fourth century, with the advent of the Emperor Constantine, and the Council of Nicea. Nevertheless, it seems that speculation about the pre-existence of the soul continued until the mid sixth century, when a crucial Council of Constantinople was held. This effectively ended debate on the subject, at least in the Eastern Church.

The preceding local synod of AD 543 also had a great and adverse effect concerning freedom to discuss this topic, for it was about the views publicised by the influential third century theologian, Origen, who clearly believed in pre-existence. [56]

Such views had some biblical support, for example in Proverbs 8.23: 'I was set up from everlasting, from the beginning, or ever the earth was.' Yet a century and a half before the key local synod of AD 543 another influential event occurred, after the Emperor Theodosius decreed in the Edict of Thessalonica, without consultation with ecclesiastical authorities, that anyone not a Catholic Christian was 'guilty of heresy, a crime punishable by death'. The lack of consultation with the ecclesiastical authorities is an important point. And, 'in AD 385, the first of a long line of reincarnationist martyrs fell.' [18] If this was indeed the case, then it would go a long way towards explaining how a commonplace and Christian belief in reincarnation might have fallen by the wayside. This latter period of persecution followed the reign of Diocletian who, as well as ordering that all churches be destroyed, declared that all Bibles should be surrendered to the non-Christian authorities. [10]

However despite these earlier and important events, it seems that the most influential gathering that affected debate and discussion about the issues of pre-destination, pre-existence, and reincarnation was the Second Council of Constantinople. It was influential down through the succeeding centuries because it was, ostensibly, such a high level and institutionally important Church forum. The Second Council of Constantinople was called by the Emperor Justinian to decide on various matters being disputed within the Church, and to assert the political supremacy of Constantinople over Rome. This Council has received much attention in connection with the subject of reincarnation because it provides perhaps the clearest evidence about what was previously believed in Christian circles about pre-existence and, separately, but linked to this topic as a matter of logic, post-existence, or rebirth.

Yet, as so often in human affairs, the influential determining factors in these matters depended on the people, or rather, personalities involved, and their psychological dispositions at that point in Church and secular history. The key personality here was not so much Justinian, but his strong-minded wife, Theodora. It was she who seems to have really made the difference to our thinking towards the subject of pre-existence and – perhaps more importantly – reincarnation.

But, to return to the events of the Second Council itself. The Pope – Vigilius – was absent from the Council, even though he was staying in Constantinople at the time. It seems that he felt under the threat of violence and, by his absence, he was making a protest about the unbalanced representation at the Council, where one hundred and fifty-nine Eastern bishops predominated, compared with only six bishops from the West. No representative from Rome was present, and it was made plain to the Pope that he was not wanted at the meeting. All this took place on June the 2nd, AD 553. [36]

This Council was insisted on by Theodora, who had a personal interest in its conclusions, for it seems that she had been sexually promiscuous to an extreme degree in her earlier years. She promoted those faithful to her and, it would appear, had her enemies put to death in large numbers, including her former sexual partners of which there were said to be around five hundred. Her husband, though Emperor, was a mere pawn in her hands. Theodora saw in the doctrine of reincarnation – to which belief in pre-existence implicitly gave rise – an inconvenient indication or acceptance that she would have to pay for her indiscretions and crimes in a future life. So she arranged for her husband to ensure that the Council repudiated the teachings of the influential theologian, Origen, who attracted her ire. [50] The outcome of the Council, denouncing his teachings, including the doctrine of pre-existence, also implicitly condemned the teaching of reincarnation. Such a change perhaps came to especially influence subsequent Western views on the subject because, less than fifty years after the Council's decision, the new teaching came to be regarded as orthodox, and by the time that Augustine crossed the English Channel in AD 597, to convert the people of Kent and some other parts of England, the prevailing Celtic form of Christianity which held sway elsewhere in much of the British Isles, and which was less sympathetic to the conclusions reached by the Second Council of Constantinople, came eventually to be overruled.

In AD 553 the Pope, not surprisingly, had initially refused to accept the decision of the Council concerning the issue of pre-existence, as it was not even unanimous, being split in the proportion of three to two. The Council could therefore make no claim to represent the view of the whole Church, and thus seems to have been little more than a sham; a Council in name only. [36]

Prior to the Second Council at Constantinople, Justinian had been asked to adjudicate in a dispute between Origenist and anti-Origenist factions in Palestine. By way of an answer, he convened a Synod in Constantinople in AD 543, which condemned the teachings of Origen, or at least those teachings which were described by its opponents. The Emperor later issued fifteen 'Anathemas' – formal ecclesiastical rejections or blights involving excommunication – against Origen, four of which were aimed directly at belief in pre-existence and, by implication, reincarnation. It is thought that Justinian submitted these proposed condemnations to a preliminary session of the unconstitutional Second Council of Constantinople, which Vigilius refused to sanction. [36] The implications of these changes may have influenced events in the twenty-first century.

An atheist commentator has stated that belief in the afterlife was the essential dynamic that made the events of September the 11th, 2001 possible.[11] However, it could equally be argued that a belief in pre-existence – and by extension to this line of thinking – post-existence,

44

might logically lead to a further life of restitution on earth as the result of causing deaths to others, and that this prospect might have discouraged or even prevented the events of September the 11th.

The birth of Islam took place within a hundred years of the events instigated by Theodora and Justinian, and this new Religion was founded in large part because of what was regarded as the declining reputation at that time, of Christianity. And Islam arose in a region of the world influenced up to that time, by the Eastern Church, and within fifteen hundred miles of Constantinople.

From a twenty-first-century perspective, it may surprise us that the then Pope had such little influence. However, in the early centuries of the Christian era, the Emperor had considerable control over the situation, not least in respect of finance. For, as a Catholic Dictionary puts it:

> in early times, the emperors, who often defrayed the travelling expenses of the bishops, were allowed to take a great part in convoking Councils. The first eight general councils were convoked by the emperors. All the later ones, on the other hand, were called and summoned by the Popes. [1]

Could it be that this powerful element of financial control was also an influential factor when the Council of Nicea was convened by the Emperor Constantine? If this is so, then it might help to explain why speculation as to the reality or extent of reincarnation that, hitherto seems to have been a valid Christian tradition, became generally excluded in the interests of establishing a particular uniformity of belief which suited the needs of the then emperor, and his empire, even though there were some Christian leaders such as Bishop Synesius, who subsequently insisted that the pre-existence of souls was a valid truth, and even that of rebirth where necessary. [27]

At the Second Council of Constantinople, personalities were very important, and especially the psychological aspects of the upbringing, and respective ages of the protagonists, for Justinian had been brought up to be Emperor, and thus had a reputation to maintain. Furthermore he was quite a lot older than Theodora who seems, initially at least, to have been his mistress. The Byzantine Emperor Justinian was born in the year AD 483, and brought up in rather austere circumstances by his mother and his uncle, the 'peasant' Emperor Justin, who rigidly groomed him to inherit the throne of Constantinople, modern day Istanbul, now capital of Turkey.

Justinian developed a great interest in the law, and he revised Roman Law to such an extent that it subsequently became the basis for Western European Civil Law. Although he considered himself to be essentially a 'good' man, he was easily swayed by flattery. He did however have a very clear grasp of military strategy implemented and perhaps especially influenced by his youthful General, Belisarius. [36]

That Justinian did not rise to achieve the posthumous reputation of a Charlemagne, was due in large part to one woman's ruthless bid for self-aggrandisement and approbation. Theodora, born in the year AD 508, was some twenty-five years younger than Justinian. According to her only contemporary biographer, Procopius, she had, before marriage, given birth to a son who, when grown up, returned from Arabia and announced his presence to her, only to promptly disappear for ever. The assumption seems to have been that his appearance was so embarrassing to Theodora, and threatening to her ardent hopes of advancement at Court, that she arranged for him to 'disappear'.

This was perhaps the most extreme example of her way of acting and operating but removing obstacles to her aim of rehabilitating her reputation became a pattern in her life and, with the help of her husband, also the changes instigated both to the law of the land and the beliefs of the Church. For, once she had become Justinian's mistress, she set her sights higher, and determined to become his Empress. And Theodora, as part of this process, wielded sufficient authority over contemporary records to suppress most of the evidence of her background which so counted against her, and her reputation.

Theodora seems to have been the daughter of a bear-feeder in the amphitheatre at Constantinople, and made her debut as a child actress when that profession ranked with the world's oldest. In this too, she became accomplished it seems. Justinian's mother objected to the developing liaison between her son and Theodora with all the power at her command, and although the law forbade men above the rank of Senator to marry actresses, that law was conveniently abolished by Justinian following the death of his mother, and Theodora took her place beside him on the throne. [36]

A former Dean of Guildford Cathedral described the situation by saying

46

that the Emperor Justin's wife, the Empress Euphemia, had been implacably opposed to Justinian marrying Theodora, but the Empress 'suddenly and most conveniently died in about the year 523'. For, so far as Justinian was concerned, now 'nothing stood in the way of his marriage to the girl he adored, except the law which forbade anyone who had been an actress from marrying a man such as himself. It was not difficult to persuade his uncle to have that particular statute changed.' [5] This seems to have been one of the main ways in which Justinian's preoccupation with matters legal started. And the route forward for both Theodora and Justinian became clearer when the Emperor Justin died four years later in the year 527. In 529, Justinian codified Roman law, which came to affect the development of law in European countries, thus coming to be known to history as 'the Lawgiver'. Then, in 532 he commissioned the construction of the Church of St Sophia at Constantinople to replace one built by Constantine the Great in 326, and designed to surpass all other buildings.

Theodora may or may not have been implicated in the unexpected and early demise of Euphemia, and after all this time it cannot be proved one way or the other. However, Procopius of Caesarea, former secretary to General Belisarius, and Theodora's biographer, so detested her, that his *Secret History* has been questioned in some academic quarters as being too critical, even though, in essence, it seems likely to be substantially true. To provide a better idea of Theodora's character, it may be worth further describing the methods attributed to her in achieving her ends. It was said that her strategy was always to create a condition of confusion in which everyone found that they were in conflict with others, thus enabling her to 'divide and conquer'. Whereas Justinian's knowledge of the psychology of others was said to be faulty and erratic, Theodora's was expert and predatory. Where he vacillated, she was as inflexible as iron.

The *Encyclopaedia Britannica* described the situation as follows:

> Officials took an oath of allegiance to her as well as to the Emperor. The city was full of her spies, who reported to her everything said against herself or the administration. She surrounded herself with ceremonious pomp, and required all who approached her to abase themselves in a manner new, even to that half oriental court. [36]

Her favourites were rapidly promoted to positions of power, and her enemies died in such numbers that the public rose up against the royal couple. Confronted by the Nika insurrection in AD 532, when Theodora was still only twenty-four years old, Justinian, terrified and demoralised, would have fled before it, but the indomitable Theodora preferred death to obscurity, and strengthened by her, the riots were finally subdued. After that, Justinian seemed hardly more than a glove puppet on her strong right hand, and she was free to concentrate her energies on the most formidable of her foes, the Church of Rome.

Theodora saw the Church as a potential and permanent monument to her own reputation, and set out to drastically revise its belief systems. That she eventually succeeded was due in large part to the fact that the Vatican had barely recovered from its subjugation by Theodoric the Ostrogoth, one of many invaders who were trying to gain influence and power via Rome, before it found itself under the 'police protection' of Belisarius's army of occupation.

The formative theological influence on Theodora, at this stage, and which suited her aim of restoring her reputation, came through her first and most influential teacher, Eutyches, a devotee of the Eastern Church. He and Theodora journeyed first to Alexandria, and then to Constantinople, he as the spiritual leader of a series of Monophysite religious schools. [36] Construction of the new church at St Sophia, dedicated to Christ, was begun in the same year as the Nika insurrection, seen perhaps at some level to be a monument to a compromise with Monophysite views – and even Theodora, representing Wisdom?

The religious cause of many of the subsequent schisms – the Monophysites

This group or sect, represented, in a sense, the philosophical cause of the religious splits that followed, though the debate which it polarised had been going on for centuries. It was this sect that was instrumental in discrediting references to the idea of 'pre-existence' and thus, by implication, 'post-existence' or reincarnation and split the Church, more than before, into two warring factions which, in differing forms and under different names, have been continuing ever since.

After all, schisms had plagued the Church since at least AD 300, after which Constantine, and the Council of Nicea, settled or, rather, endeavoured to settle splits in opinion by means of credal formulae.

The Monophysites, whose beliefs gained such influential support via

Theodora in the early sixth century, contended that Jesus's physical body was wholly divine, and had never at any time combined divine and human attributes. It seemed to cause them no embarrassment that Jesus himself had declared that there was a spark of the divine in every human soul. They believed that the act of donning the trappings of a mortal body would have defiled the true origin of Jesus.

Theodora became a convert to the then controversial Monophysite views, not least because they totally rejected those teachings of Origen which supported the concept of pre-existence. The Monophysites also put all the emphasis on Jesus and the body of Jesus being God incarnate. These arguments between the Eastern and Western branches of the Church over the extent and nature of the divinity of Christ, aroused extraordinary antagonisms in both camps, much as they do today. However, those who had argued that Jesus's body incorporated human attributes, then found themselves on the 'losing side', largely because of Theodora's influence, and the views associated with them led to the undermining of official support for the philosophical link to sympathy for the idea of reincarnation; a concept which other religions considered to be such a logical concept, particularly in terms of 'fairness'. [36]

Chalcedon – an attempt at reconciliation

An attempt to reconcile these differences had taken place before both Justinian and Theodora were born, at Chalcedon, in the year AD 451, by what was known as the Chalcedonian Decree. This protected the teachings of Origen and, to show how influential Theodora was in changing the previously held views of Justinian, one reference book records that one of Justinian's first public acts was to make the Patriarch of Constantinople declare his full adhesion to the Creed of Chalcedon. [13]

This would seem to provide solid evidence that prior to Theodora's arrival in terms of influence, Justinian was in complete sympathy with what seems to have been the Origenist leanings of the Church of Rome, or which at least did not condemn those who supported the concept of pre-existence. And if the pre-existence of the soul prior to incarnation was accepted, then the post-existence of the soul and, in some cases at least, reincarnation, could in logic be accepted also, just as some Jewish groups such as the Essenes had done. And the Essenes had close links with the early Christians, as is shown for example by the reported finding of fragments of both Mark's Gospel, and Paul's first letter to Timothy, at Qumran, now widely thought to be an Essene settlement. [12]

However Justinian's change of mind on the subject is indicated by his action in AD 543 – just six years after the church of St Sophia was inaugurated – when, at Theodora's urging, he permitted a local synod to discredit and condemn the writings of Origen. In AD 542, the bubonic plague had broken out in Constantinople for the first time in history, spreading throughout Europe. Perhaps then it was no accident that the local synod was convened just a year after the outbreak commenced, for what would happen to all those who died suddenly as a result of the outbreak, that had started in Theodora's and Justinian's home city? Would they go permanently to heaven, or would they return, perhaps not thinking too kindly of the authorities who might have allowed such a thing to happen, whether inadvertently or not. Origen's teachings, according to some people, inferred that a few, at least, might return. [60] No wonder, in such circumstances, that Justinian, with Theodora's active encouragement, might have been keen to set up a local synod at that time, with a view to undermining Origen's views on the afterlife, pre-existence, and perhaps even reincarnation.

It has been argued that 'faced with a preponderance of Origenists and other reincarnation groups' the Emperor felt that Christians might become lax, thinking they had more than one life to achieve a state of perfection. 'Give them one life only,' he is reported to have said, 'and then give them heaven or hell.' Perhaps he had come to believe in his own 'concocted doctrine' of 'give them one life'. Maybe his developed interested in law and legalities and statutes encouraged him to think that his power extended to deciding such matters. However it may have come about, this doctrine has been largely accepted as orthodoxy by Western religious belief systems today, Islam included.

How then does this help the victims of those who slaughter and kill, including those who die in wars, in the belief that they too will 'live only one life', and that, in the case of suicide bombers, they can go on to live in permanent paradise, as martyrs, for what they consider to be a 'just cause'. And, moreover, being able to do so without being able to offer any practical acts of penance or recompense to their victims.

But Theodora, it seems, felt that if, in her new position of powerful influence, she could arrange to eliminate the most obvious passages in the Bible that referred to reincarnation then her reputation in this life, enhanced by marriage to the Emperor, might be less susceptible to criticism if she was no longer seen to be in line to return to earth to pay for her misdeeds.

That biblical texts were indeed altered after the Emperor Constantine insisted on 'orthodoxy', early in the fourth century, seems to have been confirmed by Archdeacon Wilberforce of Westminster, with his comments that 'after the Council of Nicea in AD 325, the manuscripts of the New Testament were considerably tampered with.' [44]

And Professor Nestlé, in his *Introduction to the Textual Criticism of the Greek New Testament* wrote that certain scholars, called 'correctors', were appointed by the ecclesiastical authorities, and actually commissioned 'to correct the text of Scripture in the interest of what was considered orthodoxy'. [44]

The nature of the more authentic teachings, especially those which the Council of Chalcedon implicitly supported and which, with Theodora's help were subsequently rejected, would seem to be confirmed by the Early Church's first historian, Eusebius, in documents published under the heading *Origen's Cycles of Existence*, a translation from the Greek being as follows:

> Those rational beings who sinned and on that account fell from the state in which they were, in proportion to their particular sins, were enveloped in bodies as a punishment; and when they are purified, they rise again to the state in which they formerly were, completely putting away their evil and their bodies.
>
> Then again a second or third, or many more times they are enveloped in different bodies for punishment. For it is probable that different worlds have existed, and will exist, some in the past, and some in the future (Butterworth, *Origen on First Principles*). [58]

In the year 536, nearly a century after Chalcedon, two – arguably three – heroes came on to the scene who courageously stood up to Theodora, and these were, in particular, the two successive Popes, Agapetus and Silverius. Unfortunately, both these saintly men, like so many before them who had expressed their opposition to Theodora, died after so doing in a fairly short space of time. Agapetus had said to Justinian: 'With eager longing have I come to gaze on the most Christian

Emperor Justinian. In his place I find a Diocletian.' The reference here, by Agapetus, is to one of the tyrant Caesars who persecuted Christians around the beginning of the fourth century, before Constantine became Emperor. Agapetus concluded his remarks to Justinian by saying 'whose threats terrify me not'. Later that year, Agapetus was dead.

Pope Agapetus the first, a saint, reigned from the year 533 to 536. He was a member of an old Roman family, and was particularly interested in collecting books and manuscripts, and whose library was later incorporated into that of Pope Gregory the first, in his own monastery nearby. Agapetus had ordered that the Patriarch Anthimus, who had been installed on the throne of Constantinople at Theodora's instigation, be deposed, and had refused to acknowledge the right of laymen to teach in the Church. Shortly afterwards, Agapetus became ill, and died. His body was sealed in a leaden coffin, and taken back to Rome. [8]

A successor, Pope Silverius, also a saint, was starved to death, in exile, on the island of Palmaria (Ponza) in the Tyrrhenian Sea, probably around December the 2nd, 537. Antonina was said to have been instrumental in arranging this in order to avoid a 'show trial' of Silverius, in Rome. This might have been, it was said, very embarrassing to Antonina, the wife of Belisarius. It was recorded that Theodora had not accurately informed her husband, the Emperor Justinian, about what had happened. [8]

The next Pope to be involved in these matters, and who was said to be sympathetic to those who supported the teachings of Origen, was Vigilius. [56] Liberatus of Carthage maintains that:

Vigilius was selected as Pope at the instigation of Theodora, after giving the Empress a secret guarantee that he would abolish the Council of Chalcedon, and decisions made thereby, and enter into communion with the Monophysites. Subsequent to being elected, however, he resisted any change, and suffered from Theodora as a result. By the end of his term of office, Vigilius was regarded as being a faithful upholder of the Chalcedon Decree, but was reported to have been intimidated, and even imprisoned, for his views. [8]

Theodora was said to have been involved in arranging this. Could it be that Theodora, with Justinian's witting or unwitting help, had been instrumental in killing or imprisoning three Popes – Agapetus, Silverius, and Vigilius – the last of which, at the very least, supported in public the conclusions of the Council of Chalcedon, which in turn were sympathetic to the teachings of Origen?

The attack on Origen, successfully achieved by Theodora in AD 543, and confimred ten years later in AD 553, also included an attack on all those Early Church Fathers whose writings reflected their veneration of him. Copies of their works were not numerous, and could easily be located and expurgated, perhaps especially since Rome had been under the 'police protection' of Justinian's General, Belisarius, whose friend and, later, wife, Antonina, was herself a great friend of Theodora. The early Gospels, in Latin and Greek, were never at that time allowed to fall into the hands of laymen, and few monasteries would have had the courage to defy their Emperor – especially one whose wife had Theodora's reputation for retribution – and hide their original versions. [36] And Theodora, together with Justinian, is 'reputed to have obliterated' passages in the Bible 'which supported the doctrine of reincarnation'. [50]

The subject of reincarnation could thus be said to be a partial cause of the split between East and West in Christendom, formalised in the year 1054, because the split started with the dispute between Pope Vigilius and the Emperor Justinian which was signified by the Second Council of Constantinople in the year 553. Herein lies, perhaps, a potential solution or at least partial solution to the ending of the split. For mutual recognition of the historical importance and even truth concerning the subject of pre-existence and reincarnation could lead towards reconciliation between 'East' and 'West' in Christianity. And perhaps between and within other religions too, as, in part, the following chapter seeks to make clear.

6

Islam and Reincarnation

Islam is reported to revere both the Old and the New Testaments of the Christian Bible, so that many of the arguments in favour of rebirth and reincarnation described in earlier chapters of this book may be accepted by them. [56]

If indeed reincarnation is taught in the Koran, as the quotation contained in chapter 3 indicates, then the incentive for suicide bombers to take the actions they do will, to a large extent, be removed. For then they might realise that they may be likely to have to return to earth in order to recompense their victims in some practical way, instead of living, permanently, in paradise. If the teaching about the reality of reincarnation did indeed continue in the early years of Islam, then this line of argument will be strengthened.

The Islamic tradition that points to an afterlife in paradise, at least for some, followed the Christian idea of belief in resurrection, but it has been suggested that in the early Christian era, before Constantine and the Council of Nicea, the relevant verses referring to resurrection could have been intended to refer to reincarnation. [56] And it may be, as further explored in chapter 9, that 'Paradise' is not the same as 'heaven'.

Such comments about reincarnation would probably have been supported by one group founded in the eleventh century, and described as an offshoot of Islam. They were and are known as the Druze, or the Sufis of Syria, and they accepted reincarnation as a fundamental principle, and thus it was a belief which underlay much of their theology, with a reincarnation formula of recognition being adopted by them in Syria, Lebanon, and Jordan during the early middle ages, including one Druze catechism dating to the year 1012. [18]

The author Steven Rosen writes that Mohammed himself affirmed that the Koran 'had an esoteric foundation' and that 'the inner meaning of many texts included a reincarnation sensibility, but this was lost over the course of time', so that, to this day, reincarnation is generally discussed only in the Sufi tradition. [56]

The Sufis of Syria are said to have a religion that has been described as incorporating 'a blending of Islamism, Judaism, and Christianity'. Syria, and the link with Christianity – and indeed Judaism – is of especial interest because it was in Syria, at Antioch, that the followers of Jesus were first called 'Christians'. Antioch was called 'Queen of the East' because its population included people from Persia and India, in addition to which it had a large Jewish colony. [2]

Another country where the Druze had adherents, as already mentioned, was, and still is, the Lebanon. And it is here, at Mount Hermon, close to the border with Syria, that there is to be found one of the main locations associated with the transfiguration of Jesus. Mount Tabor, nearer to Tiberius, by the Sea of Galilee is usually thought to be the other location associated with the transfiguration, but this is more of a hill than a mountain, the top of which is hardly large enough for the constructions described in the New Testament to be built. The description in Mark, 9 is as follows:

> 2 And after six days Jesus taketh with him Peter, and James, and John, and leadeth them up into an high mountain apart by themselves: and he was transfigured before them.
>
> 4 And there appeared unto them Elias with Moses: and they were talking with Jesus.
>
> 5 And Peter answered and said to Jesus, Master, it is good for us to be here: and let us make three tabernacles; one for thee, and one for Moses, and one for Elias.

As mentioned in earlier chapters, the King James' translation refers to 'Elias' rather than Elijah but they are one and the same person, and Matthew 17.13, makes it clear that Elijah – or 'Elias' – had returned as John the Baptist. Perhaps then it is no coincidence that the Druze, believing as they do in reincarnation, had a particular link with Mount Hermon. And Eusebius, the Church's first official historian, in the fourth century, said that Mount Hermon was the site of the transfiguration. This is also a local tradition around the Sea of Galilee. Furthermore, local tradition refers to Hermon as 'a Holy Mountain'. [51]

This may well link with what is recorded in the biblical New Testament in 2 Peter 1:

18 And this voice which came from heaven we heard, when we were with him in the holy mount.

In Hebrew, the word 'Hermon' can be translated as 'a place set apart'. [51]

It may be that this very particular, and locally identified 'apartness' is being referred to in Mark 9, verses 2 and 4, as set out above. 'Elias', in this translation being, of course, Elijah. And it is not necessary to interpret 'high mountain' as meaning the very summit of Mount Hermon. It could simply refer to one of the peaks on the Hermon range. [51]

In G. F. Moore's Ingersoll lectures on transmigration, he is reported by Rosen to have said that 'among Mohammedans, the difficulty of reconciling the sufferings of innocent children ... with the goodness or even the justice of God, led some of the liberal theologians to seek a solution in sins committed in a former existence' and that 'reincarnation is fundamental to the doctrine of Imam as held by the [Shi'ites]'. And Muslim theologian Earl Waugh is quoted as follows:

Reincarnational notions reside in the rich texture of Islamic culture and are the product of its sophistication; they are not an 'add-on'. [56]

The Islamic historian, E. G. Browne writes about this in his three-volume work *The Literary History of Persia*. In the course of discussing some of the more esoteric schools of Islam, he describes 'three forms of transmigration accepted by classical Muslim thinkers', namely 'the periodic incarnation of a saint or prophet; the immediate return of an Imam or any other important spiritual leader after death; and the ordinary reincarnation of all souls'. His writing indicates that 'a careful study of Islam's various traditions and theological writings reveals that reincarnation is an integral part of its fundamental message to the world.' [56] If this is so, then might not the wider promotion of this teaching discourage suicide bombers from undertaking such an activity? Might it not be a persuasive argument in favour of endeavouring to resolve problems by peaceful dialogue and negotiation instead?

7

Were alterations made
to the biblical texts?

The Bible, as we have it today, is drawn largely from source material that is later than the time of Justinian and Theodora. Apart from fragments, the major manuscripts available are known as Codices, and commentators say that there are less than a dozen such documents, and the most complete Bible we have dates from a much later period, just before the tenth century. No complete Anglo Saxon Bible, or even New Testament from this period exists in the public domain.

Now if these codices were unaltered and original, this would under-mine any argument that decisions made in the mid-sixth century had resulted in amendment and affected the accuracy of the texts. However, in *Codex Siniaticus* alone, Tischendorf, who brought the text to the outside world from St Catherine's Monastery, lists 14,800 places where some alteration has been made to the text. Originally it must have contained about 730 leaves, of which only 148 are from the New Testament and which remain today. It contained the *Epistle of Barnabas*, and part of the *Shepherd of Hermas*, neither of which are in the present-day Bible. Furthermore, work on the manuscript has revealed that the writing is the work of three different scribes, one of whom was a poor speller, indicat-ing that it was written from dictation. [29]

Siniaticus is just one of about nine major codices that remain in exis-tence. Perhaps if just one of the fifty vellum Bibles that the first Christian Emperor, Constantine, ordered from Eusebius of Caesarea in AD 332 could be found, then the task of authentication would be some-what easier. But all these Bibles have disappeared, so far as we know, though *Vaticanus* does date from the fourth century.

So did Theodora and Justinian, or even Constantine, arrange for the biblical texts to be altered to remove some if not most of the wording that supported the concept of pre- and post-existence, described by Origen, whose writings were praised by so many of the Early Church Fathers?

To find out, we need to look at these source documents, or codices, of which *Siniaticus* is the most recent in terms of rediscovery. Other important ones include *Codex Alexandrinus, Codex Bezae*, and *Codex Vaticanus*.

Of these, the first two, at the time of writing, are on display in The British Library, near Euston Station, in London, within the John Ritblat Gallery, and members of the public can see two pages of the open books on view. One striking aspect of these documents, is how well they have been preserved, and how clear is the manuscript writing. Whatever other reason there may be for not having many early documents for us to study in the twenty-first century, the inability of documents to survive without crumbling after some fifteen centuries is not one of them.

In the case of *Codex Alexandrinus*, a number of pages are missing, including the pre-fixed table of chapters, and twenty-five leaves from Matthew's Gospel. Although this is an early fifth-century manuscript, written on vellum, and thus originally written before the declaration at Chalcedon, nevertheless it was in the possession of the Patriarch of Constantinople in later times, and was probably brought to Alexandria from Constantinople in 1308. Originally this codex was larger, but the first *Epistle of Clement* was edited from it. Further information on this may be obtained from H. J. M. Milne and T. C. Skeat's *Scribes and Correctors of the Codex Siniaticus* (1938), at least in respect of the manuscript from St Catherine's.

The *Codex Bezae*, is of uncertain date, though is thought to have. been compiled at some point between the fourth and the sixth centuries. In other words it might have been written after the time of Justinian and Theodora. It is a bilingual, Latin and Greek document, but the Latin is not a direct translation of the Greek text, and the Greek itself contains many errors and the work of several correctors is evident, according to reference books. [13]

Codex Vaticanus is a fourth-century manuscript of the Greek Bible, and is now in the Vatican Library, but its earlier history is unknown. It was extensively 'restored' prior to the fifteenth century, and the Pastoral letters are missing. If what are usually thought to be the earliest Christian documents are missing, what else might be missing? Of the various codices currently extant and known about, however, this codex is probably the finest, but of the approximately 820 original leaves, only 759 remain. This is the earliest reasonably complete document and had a particular influence on the Revised Standard Version of the Bible. [13]

There are also relatively early codices such as *Codex Amiatinus* which is the oldest existing manuscript of Jerome's Latin Vulgate translation, that reference books describe as a primary witness to the text. However, it was written in post-Justinian times at either Wearmouth or Jarrow, in the north east of England, between the years 690 and 700. [13]

Codex Ephraemi ('C') is a fifth-century Greek manuscript of the Bible, but only parts of the original document have survived, and the text is not always decipherable.

Codex Fuldensis is interesting in that it was written in Justinian and Theodora's time, between 541 and 546, just before her death, in the manner and form of a single Gospel – not four – as was the case with Tatian's *Diatessaron*; though the text has been revised to agree with that of the Vulgate, and an annotating hand has been identified, possibly that of the eighth-century St Boniface, originally from Crediton, in Devon. [13]

Might the *Codex Fuldensis* reflect the views of Theodora, and the revised views of Justinian, later confirmed at the Council of Constantinople? Would it not be easier to disguise any change to the text of the four Gospels if it were recast in the style of a single, unified Gospel? After all, historically, a single Gospel had a good pedigree in that Matthew and Luke were said to have used a lost source document quite independent of the material found in Mark, and this, single source document is known by historians as the Book of Q; Q being shorthand for *Quelle* which means 'source' in German. The question of whether a unified Gospel still exists is discussed in later chapters.

8

Some biblical texts indicative of pre-existence or reincarnation

Even if it is accepted that biblical manuscripts were corrected during or around the time of Justinian and Theodora, does this mean that there are no passages in the Bibles we have today, that are indicative of acceptance of the concept of pre-existence or reincarnation?

It would seem not, as the following quotations from the Authorised, King James translation – the most popular version used in the USA, and quoted here because of its familiar and poetic qualities – may serve to show, though the first quote uses the Revised Standard Version to provide clarity in the last verse. Some of the passages quoted may overlap, and thus be somewhat repetitious, but this helps to emphasise the authenticity of the particular teaching. To begin with Mark 9:

11 And they asked him, 'Why do the scribes say that first Elijah must come?'

12 And he said to them, 'Elijah does come first to restore all things ...

13 But I tell you that Elijah has come, and they did to him whatever they pleased, as it is written of him.'

The King James' translation refers to 'Elias' rather than Elijah but they are one and the same person in this context. The next passage is similar, but describes the link with the returning prophet more overtly; Matthew 17:

10 And his disciples asked him, saying, Why then say the scribes that Elias must first come?

11 And Jesus answered and said unto them, Elias truly shall first come, and restore all things.

12 But I say unto you, That Elias is come already, and they knew him not,

but have done unto him whatsoever they listed. Likewise shall the Son of man suffer of them.

13 Then the disciples understood that he spoke unto them of John the Baptist.

The teaching and link with the prophets of old is emphasised, though more briefly, in the third synoptic Gospel, Luke 9:

18 And it came to pass, as he was alone praying, his disciples were with him: and he asked them, saying, Whom say the people that I am?

19 They answering said, John the Baptist; but some *say* Elias; and others *say*, that one of the old prophets is risen again.

This latter remark indicated that the disciples, like many religious people of their day, accepted the principle of reincarnation in terms of spiritual essence or soul, at least for Jewish prophets. This was foretold in the Old Testament in the Book of Malachi, chapter 4:

5 Behold, I will send you Elijah the prophet before the coming of the great and dreadful day of the LORD.

One of the other Old Testament prophets whose return is anticipated in the New Testament is named in Matthew 16:

13 When Jesus came into the coasts of Caesarea Philippi, he asked his disciples, saying, Whom do men say that I the Son of man am?

14 And they said, Some *say that thou art* John the Baptist: some, Elias; and others, Jeremias, or one of the prophets.

The emphasis for 'say that thou art' in verse 14, again brought out in the King James version by the use of italics, shows the strength of feeling indicated by the general population in respect of the anticipated rebirth of one of the prophets.

Another quotation that shows that the disciples had the issue of inter-generational pre-existence or reincarnation very much on their minds, is indicated by John 9:

1 And as Jesus passed by, he saw a man which was blind from his birth.

2 And his disciples asked him, saying, Master, who did sin, this man, or his parents, that he was born blind?

3 Jesus answered, Neither hath this man sinned, nor his parents: but that the works of God should be made manifest in him.

It is notable here that Jesus did not rebuke his disciples for suggesting that the blind man might have lived a previous life. Neither did he indicate that the blindness of their child was as the result of them having done something wrong in this, or a previous life. Canon Perry considers this 'a more likely place where reincarnation may be in the background.' [49]

A question concerning the afterlife, and married couples, and possible serial frequency of death, at least in some cases, is contained in a long scriptural passage in Luke 20:

27 Then came to him certain of the Sadducees, which deny that there is any resurrection; and they asked him,

28 Saying, Master, Moses wrote unto us, If any man's brother die, having a wife, and he die without children, that his brother should take his wife ...

29 There were therefore seven brethren: and the first took a wife, and died without children.

30 And the second took her to wife, and he died childless.

31 And the third took her; and in like manner the seven also: and they left no children, and died.

32 Last of all the woman died also.

33 Therefore in the resurrection whose wife of them is she? for seven had her to wife.

34 And Jesus answering said unto them, The children of this world marry, and are given in marriage:

35 But they which shall be accounted worthy to obtain that world, and the resurrection from the dead, neither marry, nor are given in marriage:

36 Neither can they die any more: for they are equal unto the angels; and are the children of God, being the children of the resurrection.

37 Now that the dead are raised, even Moses showed at the bush, when he calleth the Lord the God of Abraham, and the God of Isaac, and the God of Jacob.

38 For he is not a God of the dead, but of the living: for all live unto him.

39 Then certain of the scribes answering said, Master, thou hast well said.

40 And after that they durst not ask him any question at all.

Jesus' first insightful comment here refers to *worthiness*, which sounds in some ways like the reference to Solomon's pre-existent goodness, referred to in Wisdom 8, verse 20. Jesus' other interesting comment in this context, is '... neither can they die any more'. Might this be a reference to more than one physical death, akin to those in respect of the prophets, and contained and envisaged in the question asked by the disciples in Matthew 16.14 for example?

The Sadducees' interest in the subject of resurrection, is clarified in Acts of the Apostles, a book which is seen as following on from Luke's Gospel, and with probably the same authorship. The relevant passage is Acts 23:

6 But when Paul perceived that the one part were Sadducees, and the other Pharisees, he cried out in the Council. Men and brethren, I am a Pharisee, the son of a Pharisee: of the hope and resurrection of the dead I am called in question.

7 And when he had so said, there arose a dissension between the Pharisees and the Sadducees: and the multitude was divided.

8 For the Sadducees say that there is no resurrection, neither angel, nor spirit: but the Pharisees confess both.

9 And there arose a great cry: and the scribes that were of the Pharisees' part arose, and strove, saying, We find no evil in this man: but if a spirit or an angel hath spoken to him, let us not fight against God.

10 And when there arose a great dissension, the chief captain, fearing lest Paul should have been pulled in pieces ...

11 And the night following the Lord stood by him, and said, Be of good cheer, Paul: for as thou hast testified of me in Jerusalem, so must thou bear witness also at Rome.

The question of the resurrection is thus debated, on separate occasions, by both Jesus, and Paul, with the Sadducees and, in the latter case, with the Pharisees as well. And, as Paul makes clear, he himself is a Pharisee, both personally, and in terms of lineage. As was mentioned in chapter 4, Pharisees believed in the reincarnation of prophets, so, consequently, an interesting question arises. Was Paul, in referring to resurrection here, also confirming that he believed in reincarnation – at least in the case of prophets?

It is also noteworthy, that after these comments described in verse 6, the Lord stood by him with words of support, with no words of criticism recorded on this subject.

Mention of the phrase 'no evil in this man' echoes another reference to good and evil in the context of particular people, in the Letter to the Romans, chapter 9:

10 And not only this; but when Rebecca also had conceived by one, even by our father Isaac,

11 (For the *children* being not yet born, neither having done any good or evil, that the purpose of God according to election might stand, not of works but of him that calleth;)

12 It was said unto her, The elder shall serve the younger.

13 As it is written, Jacob have I loved, but Esau have I hated.

14 What shall we say then? Is there unrighteousness with God? God forbid.

Why is verse 11 in brackets? Could it have been a later addition to explain the otherwise apparent anomaly of the words in verses 13 and 14? Is not Paul saying here that God preferred Jacob to Esau, even before they were born, as verse 11 indicates? If this is true, is it not indicative of the pre-existence of those souls? And if them, why not other souls too; and not just Solomon's (as described in the Wisdom of Solomon, chapter 8, verse 20, a book which is not relegated to the Apocrypha in Catholic Bibles, as there is no such distinction between Old and New Testament writings in the Latin Vulgate from which translations have been taken).

On this basis, it seems plausible that Solomon, by way of reward for having an inherently good soul, and choosing the path of wisdom, should then receive the gift of vast wealth; a reward which seems to be summarised by Paul's Epistle to the Galatians 6.7: '... God is not mocked: for whatsoever a man soweth, that shall he also reap.'

'But,' it might be argued, 'if Paul – or Peter, and the other disciples – accepted the principle and reality of reincarnation, then why did they not emphasise this teaching in the scriptural writing that has been left to us?' The answer may be that, even if the New Testament writings we now have in the Bible are all that exist, the followers of Jesus did not, or might not, have emphasised such a teaching, even if true or substantially true, because they expected the world as they knew it to come to an end in the fairly near future, and therefore there would not be much incentive for emphasising reincarnational thinking. For example, the view of Peter in 1 Peter 4.7 reads: 'But the end of all things is at hand: be ye therefore sober, and watch unto prayer.'

With this thought in mind, the disciples and Apostles put all their efforts into spreading their new teaching more widely, with Peter and Thomas and Paul especially travelling to countries far away in order to convey their urgent message. Such an understanding may be being described in Matthew 24:

14 and this gospel of the kingdom shall be preached in all the world for a witness unto all nations; and then shall the end come.

In view of what happened in AD 70, when the Temple of Jerusalem, symbol of all that the Jews held dear, was totally destroyed by the Romans, the following verses may be seen to provide at least some sort of prophetic truth if the disciples did indeed regard them as relating to their own time and to the, then, near future. The passage in Matthew 24 thus continues:

15 When ye therefore shall see the abomination of desolation, spoken of by Daniel the prophet, stand in the holy place (whoso readeth, let him understand:)

16 Then let them which be in Judaea flee into the mountains:

17 Let him which is on the house-top not come down to take any thing out of his house:

18 Neither let him which is in the field return back to take his clothes.

19 And woe unto them that are with child, and to them that give suck in those days:

20 But pray ye that your flight be not in the winter, neither on the Sabbath day:

21 For then shall be great tribulation, such as was not since the beginning of the world to this time, no, nor ever shall be.

22 And except those days should be shortened, there should no flesh be saved: but for the elect's sake those days shall be shortened.

With such an apocalyptic view being then given out, if such was the case, it is not so surprising that any views on reincarnation might not be referred to, especially when the Pharisees and Sadducees themselves disagreed with one another about the existence of or nature of the afterlife as Acts 23.8 indicates. However, not only was Jerusalem extremely badly damaged and the Temple Mount buildings destroyed out of almost all recognition in AD 70, but in AD 135, by the Roman Emperor Hadrian's edict, all Jews were excluded by law from Judaea, and Jerusalem became a Greek city, with pagan temples and theatres [10]. If Jews, unnecessarily perhaps, died on either of these occasions, would they return, according to Divine Law, whether or not they believed in reincarnation?

And what of those who died in the attacks of September the 11th and July the 7th? Might it not be possible that men – and women – who commit violence may be obliged to 'reap' by returning to earth to make good the damage they have caused? Another quotation that provides food for thought in this context is Psalm 126:

5 They that sow in tears, shall reap in joy.
6 He that goeth forth and weepeth … shall doubtless come again with rejoicing, bringing his sheaves with him.

The concept of 'sowing and reaping' is thus emphasised in both Old and New Testaments. And the reference to 'sheaves' could refer to both skills and obligations, if the reference to them having to 'come again' is indeed indicative that some at least may need to return again to live on earth because their previous actions merit this in terms of divine justice.

This interpretation would make more sense of the passage from Revelation 13:

10 He that leadeth into captivity shall go into captivity he that killeth with the sword must be killed with the sword.

9

More recent Christian advocates of the pre-existence of the soul – or reincarnation

The Very Reverend William Ralph Inge, KCVO, DD, eldest son of the Revd William Inge, Provost of Worcester College, Oxford, and Mary, daughter of the Archdeacon of Cleveland, was Lady Margaret Professor of Divinity and Fellow of Jesus College, Cambridge, after which, for twenty-three years until 1934, he was Dean of St Paul's Cathedral. Dean Inge wrote that he could 'see no incompatibility between reincarnation and modern episcopalianism'. [43] He is also reported to have said of the doctrine of reincarnation: 'I find it both credible and attractive.' [64]

In his Hulsean Lectures, published by Longman in 1926, Dean Inge was very interesting on the subject of Justinian and Origen. He said that Justinian had attacked Origen by closing the schools in Athens that were influential in this matter, embezzled their endowments, and procured the formal condemnation of Origen. The schools referred to were those that followed Plato's teachings, which included pre-existence of the soul. However, the Dean commented that 'the Renaissance New Testament had helped Origen', presumably by publicising the existence of quotations from the Bible of the sort discussed in the previous chapter. [31]

Another well-known twentieth-century Christian who was open-minded about the subject of reincarnation was the Revd Dr Leslie Weatherhead. The biography by his son, Kingsley Weatherhead, records that he was 'President of the Methodist Church' [62] who, in 1958, explored the subject in a booklet entitled *The Case for Reincarnation*, based on a lecture given to the City Temple Church Literary Society. He wrote 'Some have felt that a belief in reincarnation is not compatible with Christian orthodoxy. If this could be substantiated, it would be a formidable indictment, but, in my opinion, it cannot.' The Revd Weatherhead pointed out that 'Christ seems to me to have referred to it as though it were part of the accepted ideas of His day. He never repudiated it, or taught that it was false.' He continues: 'Is human distress just luck then? If so, how unjust is life! But if we accept the idea that all these inequalities are the result of earlier causes, the product of some distant past, the fruit of earlier choices, then our sense of justice is preserved.' The Revd Weatherhead then goes on to quote the passage from Galatians, 'Whatsoever a man soweth, that shall he also reap', and adds: 'The matter is not usefully thought of in terms of rewards and punishments, but of causes and effects and refers to good as well as to evil happenings in our lives.' When this past President of the Methodist Conference was asked, 'Dr Weatherhead, can Christians believe in reincarnation?' he replied:

> I think they can. That is to say, I don't see anything in this theory which contradicts the Christian position. In our Lord's time, it was part of the accepted beliefs of everybody. Indeed, it was accepted by the Christian Church until 553, when the Council of Constantinople rejected it by a very narrow majority. [63]

Dr Weatherhead faces one of the criticisms of the theory of reincarnation which runs: 'But if I don't remember past incarnations, what is the point? I might as well be another person altogether.' He responds:

> I find this objection unintelligent. What more likely than that the formation of a new body means for most people the obliteration of the memories of an earlier life? Further, we cannot remember much of our own early years. Yet any psychologist would stress their importance. Thank God we can – and tend to – forget the unpleasant. [64]

Bishop Montefiore's view on this matter was that we don't know if memories of a previous existence have been repressed simply so that finally the soul is obliged to review them and so come to terms with former behaviour. [42]

In his book *Death and Eternal Life*, the philosopher of religion, John Hick, indicated in the course of his review of the subject that he thought it quite possible that Christianity would come to accept the idea and concept of reincarnation, pointing out that many other concepts which, in one era were considered not acceptable, later came to be accepted as part of mainstream Christian thinking. [30]

A number of clergymen and senior churchmen have written with varying degrees of sympathy about the subject from a Christian and biblical perspective in *The Christian Parapsychologist*, the Quarterly Journal published by the Churches' Fellowship for Psychical and Spiritual Studies (CFPSS), and edited by Canon Michael Perry. Although patrons of the CFPSS are not committed to accepting any views expressed in the Fellowship's publications, the list of patrons includes the Most Revd & Rt Hon. David Hope, former Archbishop of York; Lord Rees Mogg, the Roman Catholic; former Bishop of London, the Revd and Rt Hon. Monsignor Graham Leonard, KCVO; and, until his death in May 2005, the Rt Revd Hugh Montefiore, former Bishop of Birmingham, who spoke with sympathy about aspects of this subject from a Christian point of view in a talk given at a meeting of the London branch of the CFPSS.

In his address, Bishop Montefiore, who from 1967 was a member of the Archbishops' Commission on Christian Doctrine, said: 'So is it wrong for a Christian, and a bishop, to be investigating this subject? Surely not.' He concluded:

It is right to follow the truth wherever it may lead and at whatever cost it may entail. In fact the Church has never officially condemned reincarnation, though the Council of Lyons (1274) and of Florence (1431) implied it by affirming that departed souls go immediately to heaven, to hell, or to purgatory. Many Christians hold to the concepts of Lyons and Florence. Our ultimate destiny is reached at the moment of death, and there's an end to it, they would say. Our one proper and only goal is heaven. Yet the concept of purgatory has modified this belief. Few of us are saints. Most have good as well as evil within them, and may well need an extended pilgrimage beyond their allotted span.

The title of the Bishop's talk was 'Reincarnation – the Evidence and its Relevance to Christian Doctrine'.

In his book *Looking Afresh* [42], there is a chapter entitled 'The Nearly Last Things' in which Hugh Montefiore wrote that:

Fundamentalist Christians hold that when we die, we sleep until the Last Judgement after which we are raised up to heaven 'at the last day' with new spiritual bodies (or sent down to hell). Others hold that, apart perhaps for great saints, the rest of us who aspire to heaven need further training to be fit for this immense inheritance.

He expresses a preference for the Eastern Orthodox concept of *theosis* or divinisation whereby training is received 'to make us less immature and more godlike' so that 'we may progress from being made in the image of God to be made in the likeness of God'.

Bishop Montefiore goes on to ask whether, before entering the presence of God, 'God sends some souls back to earth reincarnated in different personalities so that they make more progress here on earth towards the goal of heaven, or, for the more advanced souls, so that they may assist others making their earthly pilgrimage?' He goes on to report that he consulted Professor Henry Chadwick, an expert on Church history, who replied that: 'There is no decree of an ecumenical Council known to me which explicitly outlaws belief in the transmigration of souls.'

Hugh Montefiore adds the interesting point that 'for all we know, persons might be reincarnated in planets unknown to us elsewhere in our universe, or in other universes where life is different from our carbon-based existence.'

As an aside, the question about whether life exists elsewhere in the universe, and if so, whether there is any evidence for this, gave rise to a fascinating comment made about an experiment made in this connection, which was described in a talk given by the author John Michell. He said that a few years ago, messages were transmitted into outer space by various radio telescopes, describing life on this planet, including the DNA of humans, and giving an outline of their appearance. One of these tele-scopes was, and is, located at Chilbolton, near Andover, in Hampshire, England, in an area of the country where 'crop circles' have been appearing in fields of wheat and other crops in recent summers. Photographs taken from planes and helicopters flying overhead have shown these crop circles featuring increasingly intricate patterns produced by the flattened wheat, including ones in which, it seems, the DNA of the sender has been given, as set out in the crop circle, 'in binary script'. The speaker showed a slide transparency of a crop circle which featured the very clear and dis-tinctive outline of an 'ET' or extraterrestrial face. It was so impressive, that when shown, it produced a sharp intaking of breath, or 'gasp' of surprise, from the audience. The crop circle, like the majority of others shown, had been produced, in all its great intricacy, with great precision, and was clearly not the product of 'Doug and Dave' type hoaxers. This particular circle appeared in a field containing ripening crops next to the radio station at Chilbolton.[13]

The views of Bishop Montefiore, suggesting the possibility of persons being incarnated on other planets may be compared with the speculation about life elsewhere in the universe in other forms, made by Edward P. Echlin, the Catholic theologian, who mentions the reference to 'all things' being created in Christ, and that 'also we include the possibility that other life may exist, had existed, or someday will exist' on other planets, or elsewhere in the galaxy. He argues that we should be open to the possibility of the existence of extraterrestrials. Dr Echlin says that historically, Christians who were open to the possibilities of stellar life included one of the Early Church Fathers, Clement of Rome, at the end of the first century AD, and also Ireneus. [17] Others who he lists as being open to the idea of life on other planets, include names of several Early Church Fathers who were sympathetic to the idea of the pre-existence of the soul, such as Clement of Alexandria, Origen, and Jerome, who translated the Bible into Latin, as previously mentioned.

However, to return to other questions raised in Hugh Montefiore's book, he reflects in even more ecological terms on the comment made by Jesus to the penitent thief on the cross, as recorded by St Luke: 'Today shalt thou be with me in paradise' (Luke 23.43), by explaining that 'the Greek word *paradisos*, transliterated here as paradise, means a garden, which suggests some future sphere which is not yet heaven itself,' adding: 'In near death experiences, it is not uncommon for people to find themselves in a garden.'

This suggestion that 'paradise' may *not* be a permanent 'heaven' is especially important if it applies to those who cause the unexpected and premature deaths of others, and especially of themselves, who, instead of going to live in a permanent paradise, in fact may find themselves in only a temporary 'other world' or temporary 'paradise', with an obligation to return to earth to make good any damage caused. This and related points were explored further in chapter 6.

Hugh Montefiore takes the view that there is 'a positive advantage to belief in reincarnation' by pointing out that 'Christians have never come to terms with problems concerning the future destiny of those who die in infancy or early childhood.' He says: 'an infant's brain is not yet fully formed. The character is not yet fully set. The infant has had no chance to mature into a fully formed human person', and goes on to ask the pertinent question in these circumstances: 'What is the future destiny of such an unformed personality after death?' and adds further: 'How can they make full relationships with others and with God? They have not yet developed sufficiently to do this. It would seem in accordance with natural justice that they should be reincarnated in another body' and commented that it is interesting that '51 per cent of young children claiming to have lived former lives assert that they died by violence when young.' Would, therefore, this apply to the young – if they were indeed 'young' – perpetrators of the violence on September the 11th, and other and subsequent acts of violence? And if so, would it perhaps apply to their young – and even their not so young – victims?

Bishop Montefiore brings his views on this subject towards a conclusion by saying: 'It seems that reincarnation is both compatible with the Christian faith, and also supported by excellent if not conclusive evidence.' This seems to concur with the views of the Revd Dr Weatherhead.

Such a teaching is hardly dissimilar to that of one of the early Christian saints, St Gregory, who lived between the years AD 252 and 332, co-terminus, very approximately, with Constantine, the first Christian Emperor. St Gregory wrote: 'It is absolutely necessary that the soul should be healed and purified and if this does not take place during this time on earth, it must be accomplished in future lives'. [43] Now if Gregory, a Christian saint, taught this during the lifetime of the first Christian Emperor, Constantine, this seems to provide an indication that such teaching was omitted from the 'official' Church teaching at the time of the Council of Nicea, perhaps in the interests of what was then seen to be required as a uniform 'orthodoxy' and codification, in the interests of 'Empire', rather as Justinian was to do, just over two centuries later.

The Revd Dr Leslie Weatherhead, one of the three best-known Methodist preachers of the last century, and not only in Britain, was a Doctor of Divinity from Edinburgh University, who suggested a variation on the views expressed by St Gregory, as outlined above. 'I think', wrote Dr Weatherhead, 'it possible, not that *all have* to come back, but that *some* have to, and that many *may* be allowed to return when it dawns on them that such is for them the path of progress. They will doubtless choose in a way which gives them maximum opportunity. Bach was born into a very musical family, but why put this down to heredity when many great musicians have had unmusical children. The soul may determine the heredity as much as heredity determines the soul.' [64]

This reference to the soul in such a context was also made, anonymously, by 'a clergyman of the Church of England', early in the twentieth century, when he wrote, in his book *Reincarnation and Christianity*, the following question: 'Why are some people happy, some miserable? Is there any hypothesis which solves the difficulty? One: the pre-existence of souls.' He goes on to mention that Justin Martyr expressly speaks of the soul inhabiting more than one human body, and that Clement of Alexandria was also said to have held this doctrine; and that 'Arnobius Rufinus in his letter to Anastasius says that this opinion was common among the primitive Fathers of the Church. The Latin Fathers Synesius, Nemesius, and Hilarius, defend pre-existence [of the soul].' Synesius especially, said the author, 'has written some very beautiful books and hymns on the subject.' Indeed, Synesius, Bishop of Ptolemais, one of the Fathers of the Church, together with Nemesius, and Hilarius, openly defended pre-existence, and made it a condition of the acceptance of his appointment as Bishop, that his views on the subject be accepted. [27]

The author of *Reincarnation and Christianity*, the only book on the subject in Lambeth Palace Library, also commented more generally on why a change to the acceptability of views such as these, had taken place. He continued:

> There is a very general opinion that the doctrine of Origen on this subject was condemned formally by the Church, but this turns out not to be the fact. The opinions of Origen were condemned by a local synod held at Constantinople in the year 543; not, as was long believed, by the fifth general Council of Constantinople (as mentioned in Robertson's *Church History*, vol. I, page 157). This is a point of very great importance to many Christians. [11]

'Jerome (in his *Epistle to Avitus*),' he added, 'and Augustine (in *Opera*, I, 294) have passages which indicate that they held this theory in part.'

In the seventeenth century, Joseph Glanvill, who was chaplain to King Charles II, wrote in his *Lux Orientalis*:

73

Few speculative truths are delivered in Scripture but such as were called forth by the controversies of those times; and Pre-existence was none of them, it being the constant opinion of the Jews ...

Every soul brings a kind of sense with it into the world, whereby it tastes and relisheth what is suitable to its peculiar temper ... What can we conclude but that the soul itself is the immediate subject of all this variety and that it came prejudiced and prepossessed into this body with some implicit notions that it learnt in another? [28]

Friedrich Schleiermacher (1768–1834) has been described as a major reformer of Protestant theology, and one of the greatest theologians of the Evangelical Church of that time. In the second of his *Talks on Religion*, published in 1799, he said:

History, in its essential meaning, is the highest aspect of religion ... For here you observe the return of Spirits and Souls ordinarily regarded as mere tender, poetic imaginings. In more than one sense we have (in this conception of metempsychosis) a wonderful arrangement of the universe, enabling us to compare the different periods of mankind on the basis of a reliable measure. For after a long interval, during which nature could not produce anything comparable, an excellent individual will return, recognised only by the Seers, and from the effect this individual produces they alone can judge the signs of the different cycles ... A genius ... will awaken from his slumber, appearing on a new scene. His speedier growth, his broader exertions, his more beautiful and powerful body, shall then indicate by how much the climate of mankind has improved, and is better adapted to the nourishing of noble growths. [28]

In a book published in Italy, in 1911, the author, Attilio Begey wrote of the Roman Catholic Archbishop Passavalli's (1820–1897) views on the subject. He recorded that this senior prelate accepted 'the truth of pre-existence and reincarnation' at the age of sixty-four. The book said that 'he lived up to the age of seventy-seven, unshaken in his conviction that he had already lived many times on earth and that he was likely to return.' He remained an Archbishop until his death. [28]

Dr Arthur Shepherd (1885–1968), Canon of Worcester Cathedral, said in his lecture, 'Christ and the Modern Man':

> If we take into our unprejudiced thinking the picture of reincarnation as the process of human evolution, we shall find in it the answer to the problems of the new world situation … the apparent inadequacy of a single earth life, or its bondage to physical or mental or moral or circumstantial deficiency, is given new hope and understanding in the realisation of the process of reincarnation. [28]

Michael Perry, Archdeacon of Durham, in an article entitled 'Reincarnation – a Christian option?', published in the *Epworth Review* of May 1983, wrote:

> Reincarnation does not appeal to me. But I should like to think I am open enough to consider the possibility that there are forms of reincarnationist doctrine which might be consistent with Christian truth. [48]

However in a more recent publication, Michael Perry does find the subject having sufficient appeal for him to refer to 'the monumental work of Dr Ian Stevenson of the University of Virginia' who has 'for the last thirty years been investigating cases of children who seem to have retained memories of previous lives.' Certainly the cases collected by Dr Stevenson contain more than their fair share of people who seem to have reincarnated after fatal accidents. Christians in past ages used to teach the necessity of preparing for death in a responsible way. The old Book of Common Prayer asked that we might be spared from 'battle, murder, and sudden death'. Could it be that the danger of return is greater for those who are not ready for the life of whatever world there may be to come?

Might the findings of Dr Stevenson, and the conclusions of Canon Perry, as he now is, have relevance for those who died so suddenly on September the 11th, 2001, and July the 7th, 2005? Might those who didn't want to die be especially likely to be given the opportunity to reincarnate? And those who caused the deaths; are they really to be allowed to avoid any consequences for their actions in making reparation for the agony they caused?

In his book *The Reincarnation Controversy*, Steven Rosen quotes Hans Kung, a prominent contemporary Catholic thinker, as asserting that 'it should be seen as a central issue of Christian theology.' [56]

Hans Kung, described by his publishers as one of the most distinguished and highly regarded theologians in the world, has commented that

Christian theologians generally scarcely take the question of reincarnation or migration of souls seriously, at least at present, but has written that:

A truly moral world order necessarily presupposes the idea of *a life before the present life*. For how can inequalities of opportunity among human beings, the confusing diversity of moral dispositions and individual lots, be satisfactorily explained, unless it is assumed that the person has caused his present lot in a former earthly life by his good or evil deeds? Otherwise I would have to ascribe everything to blind chance or to an unjust God, who allowed the world to become what it is now. Reincarnation or rebirth provides an explanation for a human being about himself, his origin and future, and a justification of God.

Kung goes on to say that 'A truly moral world order necessarily presupposes the idea of *a life after this life*. For how is the expiatory balance of deeds rightly expected by so many people otherwise to be properly undertaken in a practical way,' and he then gives the example of murderers and their victims. 'How', he continues, 'is a human being to reach the development of the necessary ethical perfection in his life, unless there is the opportunity of a further life? Must there not be reincarnation therefore both for the proper recompense of all works – good and bad – and for man's moral purification?' [34] said this theological adviser to the Second Vatican Council. [14]

After considering various questions and difficulties that would arise should such a doctrine now come to be accepted, he was nevertheless able to say 'Is Christianity really incompatible with the idea of reincarnation? Cannot the latter be ... integrated into a Christian context, as so many new doctrines have been integrated in the course of the history of the Church and of theology?' [34] Interestingly, Pope Benedict XVI has recently met Kung for friendly talks on 'ethical issues'. [14]

Geddes MacGregor, who was at one time a Senior Assistant at St Giles, Edinburgh, Scotland, to the Dean of the Chapel Royal there, and who was Special Preacher in many pulpits including St Paul's, and Westminster Abbey, wrote in his book *Reincarnation as a Christian Hope*, published in 1982:

The promise of resurrection is a form of reincarnation. Origen, probably the greatest scholar of his day, was a prominent exponent of the pre-existence of the soul. What he and others say shows at least how lively a question it was amongst Gentile Christians of the second and third centuries. [39]

In a meeting held at the Albert Hall, Leamington, The Venerable Archdeacon Colley, Rector of Stockton, Warwickshire, said he was chairing a talk on the subject of reincarnation being held there, because he was hoping 'to learn what may help to resolve' a few of the perplexities of life, including 'why some live to the ripe old age of my dear father (who built this Hall for temperance and philanthropic and religious uses), while others live but for a moment, to be born, gasp and die: why some are born rich and others poor; some gifted with mentality; others pitiably lacking capacity. Then, as a clergyman, I have in my reading noted texts of Holy Scripture, and come across passages in the writings of the Fathers of the Early Church which seem to be root-thoughts, or survivals of the old classic idea of reincarnation.' The Archdeacon then referred to some of these biblical passages, including Jeremiah, chapter 1:

4 Then the word of the LORD came unto me saying,
5 Before I formed thee in the belly I knew thee;
   and before thou camest forth out of the womb I sanctified thee,
   and I ordained thee a prophet unto the nations.

The Archdeacon then mentioned Jesus' view that John the Baptist was indeed Elijah, as prophesied in Malachi (and described in a previous chapter) and pointed out the similarities of description, concerning Elijah, in terms of clothing, as described in the 2 Kings, chapter 1:

8 He was an hairy man, and girt with a girdle of leather about his loins.
   And he said, It is Elijah the Tishbite.

Whilst John the Baptist was described in the following way in Matthew's Gospel, chapter 3:

4 And the same John had his raiment of camel's hair,
   And a leathern girdle about his loins.

Their home, said the Archdeacon, was the solitude of the desert. Elijah journeyed forty days and forty nights unto Horeb, the Mount of God in the wilderness of Sinai (1 Kings 19.8), whilst John the Baptist was in the wilderness of Judea, beyond the river Jordan (Mark 1.4–6). Archdeacon Colley went on to say that 'Origen, one of the most learned of the Fathers of the Early Church, says that this declares the pre-existence of John the Baptist as Elijah before his decreed later existence as Christ's forerunner.' The Archdeacon also referred to Origen's commentary on the text in Malachi, chapter 1, where the LORD said to Israel:

3   And I hated Esau, and laid his mountains and his heritage waste.

And Romans 9.13 (already described), about Jacob and Esau. The Archdeacon said that it would be unjust of God to say that the elder brother should serve the younger, without a cause, which the concept of pre-existence might indicate and thus justify.

In his long introduction to the talk that followed, he also referred to God who 'hath chosen us in him before the foundation of the world' (Ephesians 1.4), linking this to Origen's comment that 'this suggests our pre-existence ere the world was', and mentioned that Jerome agreed with Origen about this, commenting on 'the necessity of again having material bodies' before, as the exhortation in Matthew 5.48 puts it about us, said the Archdeacon, 'Be ye perfect, even as your Father which is in heaven is perfect.'

Following this introduction by the churchman, the speaker for the evening, Annie Besant, presented 'part of the evidence available from Christian antiquity as to the doctrine of reincarnation as held in earlier days, suggesting that the doctrine had "simply slipped out of sight during the days of ignorance, so that modern Christians have lost sight of part of their heritage," an idea which was really once committed to the saints.'

She then made the interesting point that the doctrine of the pre-existence of the soul, and the doctrine of reincarnation had branched out into two separate lines in early Christian writings:

Pre-existence comes forth from God, including spirits which are not incarnate in human form, and which passed through various stages, and various worlds until some of them came into the physical world, where they underwent a training. This training prepared them for a higher evolution, gradually climbing back with the experience that they had gathered, into the original purity that they had lost. That doctrine – of pre-existence – may be said to be universal, both among the Jews, and the Early Church.

However:

the more precise form of reincarnation – that is of repeated rebirths into the physical form of man on a physical earth – you find in some of the writings of the Church, but not all. Some speak vaguely of pre-existence, others definitely of repeated births into the world. But in both, the principle is the same; the idea that the human spirit coming forth from God is not inherently holy save by its derivation from the one Supreme Holiness. When the spirit has lost its primitive innocence, then it is spoken of as the soul – the soul being the intermediate state between the spirit and the body; that which gathers experience; that which passes through the various worlds in the Universe, and returns ultimately with the experience it has gathered to its primal home in God.

The speaker said that in considering the views of the Church Fathers, there was one particular form of the doctrine then 'current among the Greeks and the Romans, in the literature of their time, that they bitterly criticised; and that was that the human soul can pass into an animal form. That view, they denounced strongly and vehemently; but the very fact that it is the only form of pre-existence and reincarnation that the Church Fathers denounced, makes all the stronger their general acceptance of the principle.'

The speaker then asked her audience – including Archdeacon Colley – to therefore 'distinguish between the view of pre-existence or reincarnation as accepted in the Early Church, compared with the view expressed by pre-Christian philosophers, that the soul, once having reached the human state, could pass into an animal, in a subsequent incarnation.' She was not commenting on whether the Greek philosophers were right or wrong in that assessment, but simply stressing that this was the only form of metempsychosis objected to by the Church Fathers, and agreed with Archdeacon Colley that 'several of the Church Fathers regarded the statement from the Old Testament in Jeremiah chapter 1, verse 5, as evidence that pointed to the pre-existence of the soul', and that both Origen and Jerome regarded this statement – i.e. 'Before I formed thee in the belly I knew thee' – as one of the proofs from Holy Scripture of the pre-existence of the soul. [60]

The speaker who gave the above mentioned talk, Annie Besant, though subsequently better known for being a theosophist than a Christian activist, nevertheless considered herself to be a Christian in her youth, and married a clergyman, and she presents a fairly extensive explanation of how the belief in pre-existence was distinguished from and emphasised by the Early Church, more than the doctrine of reincarnation. She argued that Origen accepted the principle of reincarnation, and not just pre-existence, more than is generally thought, saying for example: 'The nature of all rational souls is the same, as one lump of clay' that 'God, according to the previous grounds of merit' shapes to honour and dishonour. [60] This is a somewhat similar quotation to the one mentioned in chapter 3, and the emphasis on the word 'merit' is worth noting, as this would make sense in terms of the concept of pre-existence and reincarnation.

This was not the first time that the Churchman who chaired this meeting had expressed, in public, an interest in this subject. For, more than ten years earlier 'on the Sunday of August the 18th, 1893, Archdeacon Colley, formerly Curator of St Mary's, Portsmouth, preached a sermon on reincarnation from the pulpit of Christ Church, Leamington', Warwickshire. [23]

There may, however, in some cases at least, be instances where future reincarnation does not take place, even if pre-existence is proved, according to a book quoted by the chairman of a branch of the Churches' Fellowship for Psychical and Spiritual Studies. In response to a question asked about the distinction between the two, the answer given was: 'It is possible to return to earth, but it is not usual. What is possible, is to live a life on other planets if desired.' That this was a rather difficult concept to grasp 'is because on earth one gets a very limited view of life and the universe.' and thinks 'any form of life impossible other than our own.' Whether this is accurate information or not is, of course, a matter for conjecture. [57] Another unconventional, even revelatory, book rather confirmed this understanding by indicating that whilst reincarnation back to the earth plane is possible, at a spiritual level it is not advised, not least on the grounds that it is claimed that every person who reincarnates prevents another soul from having an existence on this planet, granted by God. [7]

It is not the purpose here to write about expectations of meeting up again with a loved one in heaven or indeed other worlds, nor whether belief in or acceptance of a doctrine of reincarnation would affect this reassuring – in many cases – hope. Perhaps it may be left for others to write about this aspect, though if reincarnation, rather like gravity, is a reality – a law of nature – it may happen whether we wish it or not, as the case may be.

No list of those who have contributed to this subject whilst being an active member of their church, would be complete without reference to the Sunday School teacher, Edgar Cayce, a one-time Methodist who read the Bible completely every year of his adult life. Born in 1877 in the USA, he spoke in great detail about the subject of reincarnation as a topic preached about in biblical times, when he was hypnotised in order to treat a medical condition. Cayce was a committed Christian, and as a result of what he, to his own astonishment, said about reincarnation whilst under hypnosis, he subsequently wrote and spoke extensively about the subject in a way which helped many others recover from illness that had afflicted them, and continued to do this throughout the rest of his life. [36]

But what did Edgar Cayce, this churchgoing Christian, believe about the soul? In a talk that he gave to an audience in February 1934, he said: 'I believe that when God breathed into man the breath of life, he became a living soul. The spirit of God is life, whether in a blade of grass or in man. The soul of man is individual, and lives on.' [9]

This view about a soul surviving death, may be the one referred to in Psalm 116:

8 For thou hast delivered my soul from death, mine eyes from tears, and my feet from falling.

The term 'man', of course, was intended to be generic, and thus refers to both men and women.

Cayce, in this particular talk, continued: 'Then God reasoned with man that he must leave the Garden lest he partake of the tree of life and live forever.' Perhaps this point is the one mentioned in Genesis 3:

22 And the LORD God said, Behold, the man is become as one of us, to know good and evil: and now, lest he put forth his hand, and take also of the tree of life, and eat, and live for ever.

'What did that mean?' asked Cayce. 'Just that? Or had Satan been correct when he said, "Ye shall not surely die if ye partake of this fruit!"'? What brought physical death to man? Error!'

In this talk, Cayce commented that 'most of us' believe the Scriptures, and that if we follow these we will come to a greater knowledge of life – that is God, and we will come to a greater concept of the extent and meaning of what life is. He then specifically referred to the subject of reincarnation, and asked the frequently asked question: 'Why do we not remember when we live again?' His answer was that, 'We do not remember because we have not been righteous enough!' and referred to what he considered to be a scriptural statement made by Jesus on this subject – that if we had His consciousness within us, He would bring to our remembrances all things from the very beginning. [9]

This may well be, even seems to be a reference to John 14:

26 But the Comforter, which is the Holy Ghost, whom the Father will send in my name, he shall teach you all things, and bring all things to your remembrance, whatsoever I have said unto you.

When, under hypnosis, Cayce was asked the question, 'What part of the New Testament definitely teaches reincarnation?', he answered, 'John, six to eight; third to fifth. Then the rest as a whole.'

This reference to the relevance of John's Gospel is especially important if only because it echoes the views of the Cathars, and the revelation received by the Reverend Ouseley, and described in chapter 11. Cayce also puts the initial emphasis on chapters six to eight, rather than the sequence that begins with chapter three of the Gospel of John that is in today's Bibles. Perhaps this is significant. In any event, potentially relevant passages in this section seem to include chapter eight in particular. For example, Jesus, when speaking in the treasury, as he taught in the Temple, and perhaps or even presumably to the scribes and Pharisees who had been referred to earlier in this chapter of the Gospel, is reported in the following way in John 8:

21 Then said Jesus again unto them, I go my way, and ye shall seek me, and shall die in your sins: whither I go, ye cannot come.

23 And he said unto them, Ye are from beneath; I am from above: ye are of this world; I am not of this world.

24 I said therefore unto you, that ye shall die in your sins: for if ye believe not that I am he, ye shall die in your sins.

This latter comment seems to refer, in part, to his listeners lack of belief that Jesus was indeed the expected one, the Messiah so long awaited. His teaching here, seems to be echoed again in:

34 Jesus answered them, Verily, verily I say unto you, Whosoever committeth sin is the servant of sin.

35 And the servant abideth not in the house forever: but the Son abideth ever.

A reference by Jesus to a previous existence might then be a logical explanation of his comments towards the end of this particular discourse, in:

56 Your father Abraham rejoiced to see my day: and he saw it, and was glad.

57 Then said the Jews unto him, Thou art not yet fifty years old, and hast thou seen Abraham?

58 Jesus said unto them, Verily, verily, I say unto you, Before Abraham was, I am.

Might this both be a reference, in verse 56, to a previous incarnation by Jesus, at around the time of Abraham? This might not seem so surprising, in view of the fact that Jesus himself had responded to questions about John the Baptist having been, or who was thought to have been, a reborn Elijah, a comment reported in all three synoptic Gospels, Matthew, Mark, and Luke (16.13; 9.11; and 9.18).

And John 8.58 may also be an echo of 1 Corinthians 15:

45 And so it is written, The first man Adam was made a living soul; the last Adam was made a quickening spirit.

– a text that had also proved popular with the Cathars – and Jesus' reference to himself being a second, or 'last Adam', seems to be confirmed in the genealogy listed in Luke's Gospel, chapter 3. This starts in verse 23:

23 And Jesus himself began to be about thirty years of age, being (as was supposed) the son of Joseph, which was the son of Heli,

and the verses go back in time to the beginning of the genealogy, until finally they say,

> 38 Which was the son of Enos, which was the son of Seth, which was the son of Adam, which was the son of God.

Cayce referred to a second segment of the Gospel according to John that might, and in the light of the message he gave should, be read with a view to finding references to reincarnation. Relevant quotations from this section might include the potentially obvious John 3:

> 7 Marvel not that I said unto thee, Ye must be born again.

Verse 7 is normally interpreted today in an exclusively evangelical sense, rather than, also, in a literal sense, but might not both meanings be true, at least in some circumstances? And might, if Jesus, for example, had put the emphasis on the 'Ye', he have meant that in the case of the person he was talking to, that he, Nicodemus, would need to be physically 'born again', as well as being 'born of the Spirit'? There then follows the rather less familiar, and perhaps more allusive:

> 8 The wind bloweth where it listeth, and thou hearest the sound there-
> of, but canst not tell whence it cometh, and whither it goeth: so is
> every one that is born of the spirit.

Verse 8 may refer to the spiritual 'law' of cause and effect, whereby events from the past, and unseen-by-human-eyes consequences perhaps extending into the far and similarly unseen future, might be what is being referred to by Jesus.

The theme of 'unseen by man' by means of normal sight, and 'sowing and reaping' also would appear to be the subject of John 4:

> 38 I sent you to reap that whereon ye bestowed no labour:
> other men laboured, and ye are entered into their labours.

The question of 'sowing and reaping' and 'labouring' may be related to the ostensibly difficult and sometimes misunderstood word 'sin', here understood to mean 'wrong thinking' or 'harmful actions'. Perhaps this is another aspect of the law of cause and effect being referred to in the passage within the second 'segment' of the Gospel that Cayce said was so important in this context.

84

The reference to 'causation' is mentioned in the following quotation that refers to the man who, having suffered from an infirmity for thirty eight years, had been told by Jesus to 'Rise, take up thy bed, and walk.' It is described in John 5:

14 Afterwards Jesus findeth him in the temple, and said unto him. Behold, thou art made whole. Sin no more, lest a worse thing come upon thee.

And the specific reference to 'sowing and reaping' has already been mentioned in earlier chapters, and is well described in Galations 6:

7 For whatsoever a man soweth, that shall he also reap.

When Edgar Cayce was asked the question: 'Does the good or evil we do now, set the scene and circumstances of future incarnations?' the answer given was 'Better get in shape so that you can incarnate!' He continued:

It depends a great deal upon what you do about your present opportunities. It isn't set from time immemorial as to what you will be from one experience to another. There are laws which govern this.

The Creator intended man to be a companion with Him. How many lives will it take for you to become a companion with Him? There is a law for that too. What you sow, you will reap. Each time, you go up or down. If you make the most of your opportunities this time, you can be sure that, wherever and whenever you appear again, you will be a better person and closer to God. [9]

This sounds rather similar to the arguments advanced by Bishop Hugh Montefiore, cited earlier in this chapter.

In answer to the question: 'Explain and illustrate the spiritual law expressed in "as ye sow, so shall ye reap"' Cayce, under hypnosis, replied: 'A study of such things will give many an individual an insight as to what is meant by reincarnated influences, or karmic influences built; for karmic influences are more of the spiritual than an earth's experience.'

And, in response to a question asked, nine years later, in 1943, Cayce said: 'What ye sow, ye reap. Apparently there are often experiences in which individuals reap that which they have not sown – but this is only the short self-vision.' This seems to link with the quotation in Galatians 6.7, mentioned in earlier chapters and above, and with Jesus' saying in John 4:

37 And herein is that saying true, One soweth, and another reapeth.

One question likely to arise in conversations with churchgoers concerning the subject of reincarnation, is: 'What is meant by the "resurrection of the body", as the expression is used in Christian theology?' Cayce, whilst under hypnosis, answered the question in the following way: 'The soul was created perfect in the beginning. It passes through the earth plane (during a sequence of incarnations) wherein it may obtain its (spiritual) body to present before the Creator.' [9]

The importance, even primacy of the Gospel of John was much emphasised by both the Cathars, and the Reverend Ouseley, during the course of the revelation received by him, as mentioned earlier. In view of the fact that many if not most contemporary theologians take the view that John's Gospel is a late addition to the Gospel writings, what then does Cayce say of the matter? In response to the question 'Who wrote the four Gospels?', his answer was, 'John was written by several (people); not by the John who was the beloved, but the John who represented, or was the scribe for, John the beloved – and, as much of the same, was written much later. Portions of it were written at different times and combined some fifty years after the crucifixion.' This view of the authorship of John's Gospel, as we have it in our present-day Bibles, being by another man whose name was John, is not one held by some translators, for example Rieu. [55] However, others say that it did indeed come from a group of St John's disciples. [10] But if Cayce's information is correct, then it is entirely possible that one of these earlier versions of John's Gospel, and perhaps even the most authentic or original manuscript, was the one taken by persecuted and fleeing Christians who travelled by boat along established trade routes to southern France, to be safeguarded, and subsequently looked after by the Cathars, until at least the time of the siege of Montsegur in AD 1244, seven hundred years before the dramatic events of 2001, in New York.

10

Environmental consequences including earthquakes

The environmental consequences of the events of September the 11th, 2001 and their aftermath may not only have implications in terms of a possible future existence for those who caused the damage, but also those who died or suffered ill-health as a result.

Some four months after the event, there were reports from campaigners[15] who said that asbestos levels in some buildings in Lower Manhattan were more than 500 times the recommended safe amount, with doctors finding people with narrowed airways to their lungs, and bronchial infections. And the Journal *Property Week*, of September the 28th, 2001, contained a letter from the editor of the *British Asbestos* newsletter, referring to enquiries about whether there was asbestos in the World Trade Centre, and mentioning that 'Men who sprayed asbestos fireproofing on and in skyscrapers and people who worked in the vicinity of sprayers have died in their thousands from asbestos-related diseases in the UK and abroad.'

These actions have consequences, but without a notion of possible future consequences, and not just in this earthly life, it is easier to accept that we can do what we like to the Earth, and the environment. When the Western mind rejected the concept of reincarnation – and even that of pre-existence – and in this context, Constantinople counts as Western – it encouraged us to develop attitudes towards the planet and our fellow creatures which are, too often, selfish and destructive. [50] Destroying and then burying previously healthy animals as a method of treating foot-and-mouth disease, in a world in which there is much starvation, may be a case in point in respect of animals.

Without fear of suffering, the lack of good stewardship – in a personal way – unnecessary waste, and even cruelty may well be the consequence, unless the social mores guarding against such action are extremely strong. In recent generations we have pillaged the planet as few generations have done before. The seas are almost fished out in many areas, and there is dumping of toxic waste both in the seas and on the land, with consequences for our descendants. If a law of reincarnation exists, at least for some, might it not be a form of divine justice that those who polluted, whether by means of asbestos, or in other serious ways, might be obliged to return to live in and experience the consequences of their former action? And this applies also to those who caused damage in the second Iraq war, for example, and those who continue to cause damage in the course of its violent aftermath.

'A tree is known by its fruits,' said Jesus, in one of the last of his teachings at the Sermon on the Mount (Matthew 7.20). Might this teaching apply to those who cause environmental damage to their own, and future generations? Future generations might indeed be affected by environmental damage caused by the events of September the 11th, 2001 and their aftermath. For example, the offspring of mothers-to-be who have been so affected. The horrors of asbestos-related diseases are now quite widely understood, and these have a long incubation period. And not just asbestos, for the air quality in Lower Manhattan was in many ways as bad as it was when soldiers from Iraq set fire to the Kuwaiti oil wells towards the end of the first Gulf War, according to a report in *The Times of London* (on February the 13th, 2002). It described a level of air pollution, according to one study, which for weeks after the World Trade Centre attacks, for a mile around the buildings contained not just asbestos, but sulphur, mercury from wiring, lead from computers and nickel from the combustion.

Under the Divine Law of justice, will those who caused such damage be obliged to return to earth to try to make good the harm caused in some way? And what of the justice of attack and retaliation by bombing as part of the battle to find the alleged perpetrators of the harm caused on September the 11th? Will they too have to make good the damage that they have caused to the thousands made homeless and who have died in Afghanistan, or indeed Iraq, as a result? Would it perhaps be divine justice if those who caused the bombing and authorised it were obliged, under this Divine Law, to return to either look after the innocent whose lives had been so disrupted, or themselves to live in circumstances of environmental degradation?

Divine consequences, otherwise known as the law of cause and effect, or 'whatsoever a man soweth, that shall he also reap' (Galatians 6.7), may also be more immediate. Just after heavy aerial bombing elsewhere in the country a powerful earthquake struck northern Afghanistan, according to newspaper reports on March the 4th, 2002. At least five people were killed and thirty or more injured in Kabul, the capital, and in the eastern city of Jalalabad, at least thirty houses collapsed. Even as far away as the Pakistani capital, Islamabad, and the Indian capital, Delhi, the earthquake caused people to flee into the streets as a result of the quake, which measured 7.2 on the Richter scale.

Could the bombing have 'triggered' this earthquake? If so, will the five innocent people who died, be given the chance to reincarnate, by a just God? And could the environmental and other harm that took place in the New Orleans area as the result of hurricane Katrina have been exacerbated by spiritual 'cause and effect' in relation to what has happened in Iraq?

On the 24th of March 2002, a further earthquake measuring 6 on the Richter scale, killed and injured thousands of people, leaving thousands more homeless. Its epicentre was about 100 miles north of Kabul, in Afghanistan. Although weaker than the quake earlier that month, it caused much more damage because it took place nearer the Earth's surface. Was this further quake 'triggered' by the massive aerial bombing campaign that took place earlier? Will the people who died be given the chance to reincarnate, and complete their earthly lives by the operation of a Divine Law?

The morality of the action of much of what has happened in Afghanistan in the months following September 2001, has been criticised by a senior Churchman, the then Archbishop of Wales, Rowan Williams, who was reported in *The Sunday Times* of January the 20th, 2002 as saying that there was little to choose between dropping bombs on Afghanistan and the September the 11th attack in New York. The Archbishop said that he thought that Afghan peasants – that were unlikely even to have heard of New York or the World Trade Centre – and who found that bombs were being dropped on them, would discover that it didn't seem very different to what happened to the people who suffered in New York.

Soil has been harmed for future generations, in New York, Afghanistan and Iraq. Will those who caused such damage be obliged to return, perhaps as committed environmentalists, to clear up some of the damage caused, or to act to find ways in which problems can be solved without, in the case of Afghanistan, mountains having to be bombed; mountains that can no longer be so appreciated as places of beauty by future generations? Can we find a way to take seriously our responsibility for stewardship of creation as described in the Scriptures? What would Jesus have said about this sort of situation? What did he say? Is there more that we can find out about the authentic Gospel teaching on this subject?

The next chapter will explore what more we can usefully learn about this, to avoid unnecessary destruction in the future.

11

Back to the future part I:
towards the truth of a unified Gospel

If we could rediscover a more persuasive and authentic way of finding out what Jesus said, and Paul and the other disciples taught, might that help to avert acts of terrorism, and environmental destruction in today's more interconnected, and in many ways more educated world?

So far as the Gospels are concerned, we rely on the four, separate, and much admired books written by the evangelists, Matthew, Mark, Luke and John, but if we could find the source documents, or even part of the source documents from which these were composed, we would be nearer the pure teaching expounded by Jesus, which could have such a beneficial effect, especially if it made more sense to people today. For many people are leaving the churches and other places of worship in order to try to find answers to the questions they ask, in a way which makes more sense to them.

In fact there may be source documents or at least parts of source documents that are available today which may or will help to lead us back to this truth. This is likely to be especially so, if the methods of analysis and comparison used by those such as Origen, are adopted, he being regarded as a giant amongst thinkers about the true Gospel teachings, by so many Early Church Fathers, and the Church's first historian, Eusebius.

But what about the existing Gospels? some readers might say. Are they not sufficient, and much admired? Especially the King James's Bible which is so much loved, and thought by some 'to be Holy Writ in a sense peculiar to itself'. Indeed the Authorised Version (AV) is in any number of ways 'just as beautiful and intelligible to us as it was to those who first heard it.' [55] However, this translation was written before the currently available and most ancient manuscripts came to hand, and even these can

91

be improved upon; and not just in terms of the modernity of the language. Indeed, too many different translations of the same words can produce confusion amongst the public, who generally would probably prefer certainty, and above all, truth.

The Authorised Version translators based their translation on the Greek text first published by Erasmus in the year 1516. Since that time, many more ancient manuscripts have become available, including the fourth-century *Codex Siniaticus*, now in London; also the *Codex Vaticanus*, and the *Codex Alexandrinus*. And perhaps it may be possible to identify even earlier documents whose contents might not be sufficiently well known.

Some meanings and passages have been improved and clarified as a result. For example, in Mark 6.20 it was stated in the AV that Herod, when conversing with John the Baptist, 'did' many things. *Siniaticus* and *Vaticanus*, however, both indicate that the word for 'did' was mistakenly inserted instead of 'was perplexed (about)'. This makes much more sense of the sentence – and the situation.

There is also the important question of what Church authorities feel able to approve, *even if* a new text becomes available which clarifies the meaning. One such example was mentioned during a talk about the Dead Sea Scrolls, and translation of manuscripts found at Qumran. A Professor at the University of Manchester, in giving an address to the Institute of Jewish Studies, at University College London, gave an example of how an authoritative text differed from a canonical text. American Catholics, in a new Roman Catholic Bible, used a scroll at Qumran that was more complete, and made much more sense of a passage in 1 Samuel 10, and duly incorporated it. However, in the second edition of their Bible, they reverted to the old, rather puzzling Massoretic text, because they realised that if they used the Qumran text, they would be using the form which had not been approved by the Committee of Catholic Bishops; whereas the puzzling text had been so approved, so could not be changed, it seems.

'There needs', said the Professor, 'to be a switch from the implicit method of understanding, to a more explicit interpretation. But the new text doesn't have to be canonical; however it can be used to explain the canonical text. This may be the best way forward.' [6]

This question of what can be approved as canonical, versus a truer text may well have happened in Early Church history, and not only in the time of Justinian. At one time, there seems to have been a single, unified Gospel, not the four separate and much admired Gospels produced in our present day Bibles. For example, the Gospel Harmony, or *Diatessaron* of Tatian. This second-century work by an Assyrian convert was used as a standard document in that part of the world until the fourth or fifth century, when it was ousted by a standard Syriac version. However 'the *Diatessaron* was systematically suppressed in the early fifth century,' reports Christopher de Hamel. [24] Now why should an early second-century unified Gospel, previously regarded as canonical, in that part of the Christian international community, be suppressed? Was it because it contained a more authentic Christian teaching going back to the time of Jesus that was, by the fifth century, politically inconvenient? Could it have anything to do with the fact that Tatian, who produced this Gospel, was a pupil of Justin Martyr, who spoke of the soul inhabiting more than one human body?

A further link with Jesus, through the generations comes from the Christian community at Edessa, whose church in the third century, claimed as a founder, one of the seventy-two disciples of Jesus. In the time of Jesus, Aramaic was the language spoken and there is evidence that Jesus spoke it. The late Professor Burney of Oxford believed that the fourth Gospel was a translation from the Aramaic, and the form of it still spoken in the Euphrates Valley is called Syriac. [29]

The old Syriac manuscript, known as the Curetonian, comprises eighty leaves of the Gospels named after Dr Cureton of the British Museum, who published them in 1858. He claimed that this version contained the actual words of Jesus in the very language in which he spoke, compared to the Greek writing from which translations have normally been taken. And Professor Torrey of Yale, was convinced that the four Gospels that we know and that have been translated from the Greek, were in fact originally composed in Aramaic. Though at one time it was thought to no longer exist, in 1888 two manuscripts were published of a translation of the *Diatessaron* into Arabic which had been made by a monk in the eleventh century.

Are there other sources that might take us closer to the true teachings of Jesus? Apart from the material in Matthew and Luke that was obviously taken, it is thought, from Mark's Gospel, the remainder seems to have been taken from another source document known as Q. But the *Gospel of*

Thomas, found at Nag Hammadi looked very much like Q, said New Testament Professor, Burton Mack, and approximately 35 per cent of the sayings in Thomas had parallels in Q. [40] Gospel summaries were said to have been carried around by the early Christians, and another document called the *Didache*, was regarded as Scripture by many Early Church Fathers. As it has been said to date from between AD 70 and 110 it is very early indeed, and may even be earlier than the Greek St John's Gospel.

Is there another way to try to find the truth of the original Gospel, as taught by Jesus, and recorded, perhaps in Aramaic, by the disciples? One other possible way, which has a fair amount of scriptural and other, more circumstantial, support is that of revelation.

A document which at one time was regarded as authentic early Christian Scripture, is the *Shepherd of Hermas*; indeed part of it was found in *Codex Siniaticus*. The *Shepherd* is a book of revelation and one which advocates repentance; in rather different style is the Revelation of St John, which is, today, part of Scripture. The Jews had a great regard for dreams, and they play a great part of the history of the Bible, from the Pharaoh at the time of Joseph (see Genesis 40 and 41), to Daniel, to Jacob, to Joseph the father of Jesus, before the Holy family fled to Egypt. So any revelation concerning the authenticity of Scripture and the true teachings of Jesus should not be taken lightly, even if it happens in modern times, and to a clergyman. However, such is the story concerning the Reverend G. J. R. Ouseley, who was appointed Curate of Warrenpoint in County Down, Ireland, in the year 1861, before being received into the Catholic Church. *The Gospel of The Holy Twelve* was, and is, according to the 'In Memoriam' introduction to the Gospel story, and set out as a form of Harmony of the Gospels in somewhat similar fashion to the *Diatessaron* of Tatian, composed of two elements. One was the Gospel narrative, taken from Christian writings and fragments which had been hidden in a monastery in Tibet, where it had been taken by members of the Essene community for safety, and there for the first time to be translated from the Aramaic. The other was the content of the Gospel, received by the Revd Ouseley 'in dreams and visions of the night'. It was also, it seems, a translation 'of an original Aramaic document purporting to be a reconstruction of the Gospel narrative'.

'A lectern would appear before him with manuscripts thereon, and as it revolved he read the papers then presented to him. In the morning he noted what he had read, remembering it clearly. The fact that in the morning he experienced heaviness in the eyes, exactly as if he had been reading all night, seemed to him a proof' that it was an out of the ordinary event. [44]

'One thing is unquestionable,' continued the 'In Memoriam' description of what had happened; 'he could not unaided by some Power higher than and above that of his normal intellect, have written this Gospel, and that such Power was of a divine nature, is manifest from its contents. At the end of the Gospel are the words: "Glory be to God by Whose Power and help it has been written".' [44]

This publication is quoted from in some detail, if only because it is a relatively modern revelatory writing, and the process by which it came about is described in more detail than is the case with older writings. However, whatever the reader's response may be to what is described above, may be judged, at least to some extent, by the content of the Gospel given to the Revd Ouseley. Because part of this refers to the question of the pre-existence of the soul, and, at least in some circumstances, reincarnation, it seems to be worth quoting from this manuscript what Jesus's true teachings were said to be on this subject. It is said to have been written by St John about the year AD 70 when he was imprisoned in Rome, and given, page by page to one he could trust. It is described as the recovered document from which the Four Gospels as we have them today, were built up. When the scroll was completed, and after the contents had been made known to the Apostles, it was taken to Tibet by the same disciple, who left it in the care of a Lama he could also trust. [44]

The following are three quotations from *The Gospel of The Holy Twelve.* Verse 2 in the first quotation, is somewhat similar to that in John 11.25 in our present Bible translations.

CHAPTER 69
THE CHRIST WITHIN, THE RESURRECTION AND THE LIFE

1 As Jesus sat by the west of the Temple with his disciples, behold there passed some carrying one that was dead to burial, and a certain one said unto him, Master, if a man die, shall he live again?

2 And he answered and said, I am the resurrection and the life, I am the Good, the Beautiful, the True, if a man believeth in me he shall not die, but live eternally. As in Adam all die, so in the Christ shall all be

made alive. Blessed are the dead who die in me, and are made perfect in my image and likeness, for they rest from their labours and their works do follow them. They have overcome evil, and are made Pillars in the Temple of my God, and they go out no more, for they rest in the Eternal.

3 For them that have done evil there is no rest, but they go out and in, and suffer correction for ages, till they are made perfect. But for them that have done good and attained unto perfection, there is endless rest and they go into life everlasting. They rest in the Eternal.

4 Over them the repeated death and birth have no power, for them the wheel of the Eternal revolves no more, for they have attained unto the Centre, where is eternal rest, and the centre of all things is God.

As the above subheading included in the text indicates, the words of Jesus reported there provide a rather different interpretation to the meaning of resurrection to the one generally taught today. But the inference concerning rebirth, and going 'out no more' and being 'made perfect', have echoes, indeed almost repeat, word for word, the quotations in the Book of Wisdom and Revelation 3.12 mentioned in a previous chapter.

Further clarification concerning how the law of rebirth may apply, is contained in the following extract:

CHAPTER 94
THE ORDER OF THE KINGDOM (Part IV)

3 There is a resurrection from the body, and there is a resurrection in the body. There is a raising out of the life of the flesh, and there is a falling into the life of the flesh. Let prayer be made for those who have gone before, and for those that are alive, and for those that are yet to come, for all are One family in God. In God they live and move and have their being.

4 The body that ye lay in the grave, or that is consumed by fire, is not the body that shall be, but they who come shall receive other bodies, yet their own, and as they have sown in one life, so shall they reap in another. Blessed are they who suffer wrong in this life, for they shall have greater joy in the life to come. Blessed are they who have worked righteousness in this life for they shall receive the crown of life.

In the text, the above words are attributed to Jesus, in response to questioning. In some ways it could, perhaps, be described as a very much fuller explanation of more familiar quotations, such as that contained in John 5:

29 And shall come forth; they that have done good, unto the resurrection of life; and they that have done evil, unto the resurrection of damnation.

Then, in almost the last verse contained in *The Gospel of The Holy Twelve*, is the following:

CHAPTER 96
POURING OUT OF THE SPIRIT

23 As in the inner so in the outer: as in the great so in the small. As above, so below: as in heaven so on earth. We believe in the purification of the soul: through many births and experiences: the resurrection from the dead: and the life everlasting of the just. The ages of ages: and rest in God for ever. Amen. [44]

The above quotation is attributed to the Apostles after 'the Spirit of God' came upon them, following Jesus showing himself alive to them, after his resurrection. It also has some echoes of the Lord's Prayer, as referred to in the latter part of Luke 11.2: 'Thy will be done, as in heaven, so on earth.'

The implication of this last quotation from Jesus, as reported in *The Gospel of The Holy Twelve*, is that it is 'the just' that will be those in receipt of life everlasting, whilst others will be in need of more 'births and experiences'.

Whatever may be thought of the authenticity of these quotations from *The Gospel of The Holy Twelve*, they do at least have a strong internal logic, and explain in a more obviously understandable way, otherwise rather difficult and obscure passages in our existing current Scriptures.

A 'Gospel of the Twelve Apostles' was mentioned by both Origen and Jerome, reports Professor Martin Dibelius, pioneer of the Form-Criticism method of New Testament study, who speculates as to which document or Gospel this might refer to. But might it perhaps refer to *The Gospel of The Holy Twelve*? Or at least that version of it said to have been originally

97

produced by St John. The striking similarity of name makes it a more likely possibility than others that have been suggested.

Jerome 'knew and cited a Gospel in Aramaic' which was in use amongst the Jewish Christians of Syria, ones described as Nazarenes, and which he, Jerome, appears to have copied out among them and translated. He also calls it the 'Gospel of the Hebrews' and hence, among scholars, it has been equated with the Gospel of the Hebrews mentioned by Clement of Alexandria, for example. However the fragments of this document do not give the impression of being translated from the Aramaic. The 'Gospel of the Nazarenes' referred to by Professor Dibelius, may be a genuine Aramaic Gospel of Matthew. [14]

There thus seem to be quite a number of Gospel documents, as described in this chapter, which point towards Aramaic sources, both for individual Gospels such as Matthew, and unified Gospel documents as the *Diatessaron* was. The Syriac link seems very important, again with this Aramaic connection, which takes us back to the speech and times of Jesus. And yet our Bible documents tend to rely on Latin and Greek, not Aramaic. When, in the year 382, Pope Damasius commissioned his secretary, known as Jerome, to revise the Bible, the Latin was revised according to 'the true Greek text' and he himself was to decide what that text was. No mention was made of the importance of the Aramaic documents.

Might there not be a way forward in an endeavour to recapture the true essence of what Jesus and the disciples taught, prior to the changes undertaken by, amongst others, Constantine and Damasius by using some of the methods chosen to arrive at authenticity, adopted by Origen, who was described in such approving terms by Eusebius, the first Church historian, and who was himself described as the most widely read scholar of Christian antiquity. Origen, after all, pre-dated the destruction wrought by the Emperor Diocletian in the year 303, when Bibles were destroyed wherever they could be found. This was the last great persecution of the Church in the early centuries. The edict ordering all Bibles to be surrendered was issued on the 24th of February, 303. [29] The influence of Constantine was felt shortly afterwards, and that of Damasius later in that century, but to recapture the truth of what went before, ways forward are described in the next chapter. Ways that could help move the world and the Church towards a safer way of being, in the face of actions, such as bombings which cause damage, and even acts of retaliation that cause further damage.

12

Back to the future part II: can a pre-Constantine analysis enhance the appeal of Jesus' teaching beyond the West?

If there is to be a move towards more authentic Scriptures, then Origen's approach may help us, particularly the method he used in formulating the Hexapla, the six-fold layout of various Old Testament translations and variants, which was such a new approach in the third century. Now the process of comparing various manuscripts is fairly commonplace when producing modern translations of the Bible, or even when preparing a Harmony of Matthew, Mark, and Luke's Gospels. However, the difference in approach today, and perhaps in earlier centuries, is that canonicity is often the template for acceptability. In other words, radical differences of interpretation would be rejected if they are noticeably different to the established canon of Scripture. Examples of this were mentioned in the last chapter, but others include the longer ending to Mark's Gospel (chapter 16, verses 9–20), which tends to be discounted and regarded as inauthentic by modern translators, yet the earlier document (by a later translation) known to us as the *Diatessaron*, contained the longer version of Mark's Gospel, yet the *later*, post-Diocletian, and post-Constantine Codices, which modern translators tend, exclusively to rely on, do *not*, for the most part include the longer ending. [29] Other examples include the rejection of the *Shepherd of Hermas*, and the *Epistle of Barnabas*, even though their content is known to originate from a very early date indeed, and certainly the former was at one point considered to be canonical, even by strict critics such as Irenaeus, and other early Christians. Like the *Diatessaron*, these writings, containing teachings of the sort that are similar in tone to those of Jesus in today's Bibles, long pre-date the codices now used and preferred for translation purposes.

The *Epistle of Barnabas* is particularly interesting because it was found contained within one of the most important biblical Codices, *Codex Siniaticus*, and within the Barnabas manuscript, according to one translation, there is a story which, if not indicative of reincarnation, does at least give some further insight, if it is indeed authentic, of the law of cause and effect, and an explanation of an action described in the Bible, which has puzzled many people. The story concerns the person who could be regarded as the Father of the three monotheistic religions – Abraham. In chapters twenty-six and twenty-seven of the manuscript translation, reasons are given as to why Abraham was apparently so sanguine about putting his only son, Isaac on the altar, when preparing to sacrifice him by means of fire. According to the manuscript translation, something similar had happened to Abraham himself, and which he had survived.

For, following an action by Abraham in the Temple in which he destroyed the statues of all idols except the one 'great god', those who were annoyed by this action, including Abraham's Father, gathered a large quantity of wood, and, having bound Abraham's hands and feet, put him upon the wood, and lit a fire underneath.

But 'Lo! God, through his angel, commanded the fire that it should not burn Abraham, his servant. The fire blazed up with great fury, and burned about two thousand of those who had condemned Abraham to death. Abraham verily found himself free, being carried by the angel of God near to the house of his Father, without seeing who carried him; and thus Abraham escaped death.' [52]

The *Epistle of Barnabas* didn't get put into the Church's canon of approved Gospels and Epistles because, centuries after it was written, it failed the 'official' test for authenticity. However, some Early Church theologians such as Origen, had an untypical approach to testing for authenticity in assessing manuscript material.

Origen's approach was different. His aim was 'accuracy'. [29] And to this end, he was prepared, unlike most recent translation committees, to consider the unusual, even if found by himself, and himself alone, more or less. For example, one of the manuscripts used by Origen in preparing his Hexapla, was a text 'which he (Origen) found in a jar in the Jordan Valley'. [29] Would the modern-day equivalent be *The Gospel of The Holy Twelve*? Could this in fact be what might be called 'the lost Gospel of Jesus'? Would a latter-day Origen consider this today, and produce a modern 'Hexapla' of New Testament writings, in order to get us closer to the true and authentic teachings of Jesus?

What material would be used in such a new 'Hexapla approach' that completely reassesses the original teachings? A beginning is already being made by the proposal to revise the Bible, and particularly, in this context, the New Testament, by incorporating Dead Sea Scroll material. Might this not be an opportunity to include other material in preparing an authentic version that was not unnecessarily restricted by the constraints of canonicity? Other material could include, for consideration in this way, the later translation of the *Diatessaron*, Syrian manuscripts, including the *Curetonian*, the *Gospel of Thomas*, the *Shepherd of Hermas*, *The Gospel of The Holy Twelve*, the *Gospel of the Nazarenes* mentioned by Professor Dibelius, and perhaps other documents not here mentioned. Many of these writings have already been reviewed many times during Church history, but have they all been completely re-assessed in the light of the Dead Sea Scroll findings, and including the evidence of *The Gospel of The Holy Twelve*? This, as has been seen, emphasises the importance of original Aramaic writing, and particularly the Gospel of John, which may have been composed far earlier than has previously been generally supposed.

In view of what has been written in previous chapters, the question arises as to whether the subject of pre-existence and reincarnation should be put back on the religious agenda, not least for Christianity. And if Christianity came to accept these concepts as acceptable mainstream themes, in some cases at least, then might not other monotheistic religions follow too? And if that happened, might we not see established a strong incentive to end the acts of terrorism and retribution that have so scarred the world and affected its environment in recent times?

Perhaps the first question to ask is whether some form of reincarnation process really does exist; not just as a theoretical belief, but as a likely, or even definite scientific fact; rather like the law of gravity, but one which is instituted as a *Divine* Law. It is worth remembering that the Earth does indeed rotate around the sun, as a definite law of nature, and not the other way round, as once the Church taught.

Looking at some of the issues mentioned in previous chapters by way of summing up, how do they stand in terms of respective strengths when tested in this search for truth?

Taking the biblical texts first, there is a fair amount of evidence of alterations having been made, but some may prefer not to consider this possibility, either for doctrinal reasons, or because of the problems relating to canonicity already mentioned. The fact that a number of mainstream Jewish traditions, including those of the Pharisees, accepted, at least to some extent, the doctrine of reincarnation, should provide food for thought. For example, in the Talmud, it is related that Abel's soul passed into the body of Seth, and then into that of Moses. However The Talmud says that there were seven 'types' of Pharisees and commended those who followed a 'law of Love'; so even *their* beliefs within this particular tradition, had variations. [16]

The Early Church also had many who accepted Origen's view concerning pre-existence, but, in the case of Justin Martyr at least, also some element of reincarnation. This was a legitimate subject of speculation, certainly until the time of Constantine and, it seems, until the time of Justinian, not least because we know that Augustine speculated about the matter around the early fifth century, and Justin, for his part, had been a central figure in second-century Christianity. And, if the Christian tradition taught by the Cathars is included, it could be said that some support for the validity and reality of pre-existence and reincarnation continued up until the time of Aquinas, and the successors to St Francis in the latter part of the thirteenth century. Going further back to the time of Jesus, *The Gospel of The Holy Twelve*, most recently, it seems, the result of revelation, states that Jesus himself taught the doctrine of reincarnation, quite overtly and clearly, as did the Essenes, who in recent times have been more and more associated with John the Baptist, Jesus' cousin, with the former accepting this principle, so that if this link is established, it would not, by an extension of logic, be so surprising to read that Jesus taught it too.

Another impressive body of evidence, combined with fairly persuasive logic is provided by a number of Christian writers and theologians who have written about ways in which reincarnation can be reconciled with Christianity. Such writers include Hans Kung, the Reverend Leslie Weatherhead, and the Rt Reverend Hugh Montefiore, a former Bishop of Birmingham.

In addition to sympathetic individual theologians, some Christian reference books leave the matter as an open question. Take *A New Dictionary of Christian Theology* for example:

102

The compatibility or incompatibility of reincarnation with Christian belief has been discussed from time to time. Resurrection and reincarnation both constitute re-embodiment; heavenly resurrection is a kind of reincarnation in another world, whilst reincarnation is a kind of resurrection in this world. But whether we have lived on earth before, should presumably be regarded as a question of fact. If and when that fact can be definitively ascertained, any belief system should then include or exclude reincarnation in response to the evidence. [54]

This seems a very sensible assessment. Another dictionary asserts: 'Reincarnation is assumed in the Bible teaching.' [19]

Then there is the significant groundswell of grassroots Christian opinion, in many cases, greater than the national average, that accepts the plausibility of the doctrine. This is not a tiny minority, but a significant minority. In some degree, they may have been impressed by the evidence provided by case studies involving hypnosis, but this approach is left at this stage for others to investigate. Some may have been impressed by the example set by the 'Cathars who believed themselves to be the true Christians.' [18] They believed in reincarnation and, interestingly, their guiding text was said to be the Gospel of John.

There would seem to be a very good case for rehabilitating the reputation of the most important of the pre-Constantine thinkers and writers who Professor Chadwick described as 'a giant' amongst Christians of this era, and who Carsten Peter Thiede, in the *Church of England Newspaper* of the 8th of February, 2002, described, together with Eusebius, as 'an eminent scholar of the Early Church', namely Origen. Eusebius, the first Church historian, wrote admiringly of him and, together with his admirable character, by reputation, he would seem more deserving of support in this present era, than the intrigues of Justinian and Theodora, whose political manoeuvrings some three centuries later did so much to blight Origen's reputation and inhibit discussion of these important questions about pre-existence and post-existence that have so many practical implications, especially for us today, in terms of terrorism and high-tech revenge, and environmental damage by way of collateral fallout.

Concerning the important question of the events of September the 11th, 2001, and July the 7th, 2005, would official acceptance of the doctrine of reincarnation by the monotheistic religions have meant that those who prepared to attack the twin towers in New York or crowded transport systems in London would not have been encouraged to do so by the assurance that they would thereby send themselves to a permanent paradise? For if the Divine Law of justice is true for Solomon, as the Bible says, then is it not equally likely to be so for those who are, or who have been described as terrorists, and bombers? And if it is true for them, might the Divine Law of reincarnation also apply to those who bomb, and cause environmental destruction, and even starvation to innocent people in the course of their retribution and attempts to find or kill the 'guilty'. This Divine Law would therefore apply to Christians and Jews, as well as to Muslims, unless they did indeed cause no harm. However, in the case of those who are harmless, there may be exceptions. For example, Solomon, as previously discussed.

The philosopher, Schopenhauer, referred to the existence of something which might come to be seen as a 'unifying principle on which Christianity and the religions of the East (can) meet'. [20] Could that principle be reincarnation? The 'East' already accepts it. If Christianity, and the other monotheistic religions could accept it, even in modified form, then Schopenhauer's principle, or at least a major part of such a principle, would have been identified. If Jesus could be shown to have taught it, then its acceptance by Islam and its loyal Muslim followers would be more likely, as Jesus is regarded as a major prophet within Islam.

Perhaps Christianity might find it easier – at least to start with – to accept again the concept of pre-existence, in broad terms. This would have biblical support in terms of the comments made about Solomon and Jacob, and also in respect of expected prophets such as Jeremiah, and Elijah. As to reincarnation, Christianity, and perhaps other religions too, might well advance the view, with some justification, that this would not apply in every case. In other words, some souls might not reincarnate, or *have* to reincarnate on this earthly plane, in the case of souls that have no more wrongs to 'right' or personally atone for, have no more lessons to learn, could or would go to what is described as heaven, or paradise, if they are indeed the same, or even to other planets [17] or elsewhere in the galaxy.

The Roman Catholic writer, G. K. Chesterton said that, 'Eastern philosophies lead to contempt for life, whereas the Judeo-Christian approach leads to contempt for death.' But in the light of the events of September the 11th, 2001, and their aftermath, including all that has happened in Iraq, is this true? The current Christian view is that the good and the bad go to heaven and hell respectively, and with a spell in purgatory for some, though there are differing denominational perspectives on this matter. But what of babies, or the mentally handicapped, especially those who die young. Do they not deserve a full life?

Jesus taught that the truth shall set you free (John 8.32). But what if the Churches are not telling the truth in this matter, albeit for the most part unwittingly? Are they willing to change what they teach, should fuller and better information come to light? As Galileo showed.

If the Churches do accept that what they teach may need to change – for example, in the light of what the Dead Sea Scrolls now reveal – might they accept in the meanwhile, that they may not have a monopoly of understanding in respect of the teachings and significance of Jesus the Christ? Could they let go of the currently taught doctrine that may no longer serve or help the world, in the light of new understanding, especially insofar as it affects the doctrine of reincarnation and pre-existence of the soul? If this new understanding could be confirmed, even to some extent, by Early Church documents and manuscripts that have, until now, been kept from public view, perhaps in the Vatican, perhaps in some monasteries, then surely now is the time to do so given the current climate of 'terrorism and revenge' around the world. A more educated public may at the present time be open to accept such changes in a way that has not been possible for centuries, or even a millennium and a half or more.

If this enables the authentic teachings of Jesus, of the Christ, to more easily reach and be understood by and help the *whole* world, would that not be an advance in understanding worth having?

It is not the intended purpose here to write in any detail about the theological ramifications of the acceptance of pre-existence, or rebirth within Christian doctrine, or indeed that of the other monotheistic religions. However, in a Christian context, it may be helpful to mention the comments of Geddes MacGregor, who expressed the view that 'without the redeeming work of Christ, we could not hope to accomplish that self-transformation of humanity. With Christ, we can, and we shall.' [38]

'Primitive forms of reincarnation must be discarded,' he wrote. 'In the history of religious ideas, outmoded formulations' are continually giving way to 'more adequate ones'. He counsels against 'ideophobics who hug ancient formulations till they petrify, yet will not tolerate new formulations that could restore and develop religious life. Each reincarnation is, of course, a resurrection. The resurrection of Christ can now be seen as a continuing process in which every rebirth "provides" a new capacity for walking closer and closer with God.'

To conclude: The early Christians were expecting Jesus to return in the near future, and therefore their teaching, including that of St Paul, emphasised teachings and theology that excluded the prospect of re-incarnation, as it would not have appeared to be relevant. The thought of coming back reincarnated into this world rather than going on to a new and unimaginably splendid other world where they could join their heavenly Lord in glory, would have been considered a very second-rate option. [49] At least, that is the way that it might have seemed then. In today's world, some 2,000 years later, a relevant Christian message would echo and reinforce what Jesus *really* taught and is likely to have known and, if *The Gospel of The Holy Twelve* is authentic, actually preached by mentioning that reincarnation did happen. If such a teaching is accepted today, that could lessen the prospect of future acts of terrorism or revenge.

Origen was said to have considered a 'Gospel of the Twelve' but did not include it amongst the authorised texts. If this is indeed the same as *The Gospel of the Holy Twelve*, why then might he have rejected it when it is so in tune with his own thinking about the pre-existence of the soul especially? Perhaps the answer might be that by the middle of the third century the canon had been reasonably well established – by Irenaeus, for example – and Origen, if correctly reported (and his views were much censored), might subsequently have decided that a gospel that overtly referred to reincarnation could not be easily reconciled with the other gospels, where such a teaching was not so explicitly stated. And if the book that Origen was said to have consulted was 'The Testament of the Twelve (Patriarchs)' then this seems to be a quite different Old Testament manuscript set in the context of the book of Joshua, rather than a New Testament one.

However, the most important re-emphasised teaching from Jesus, and the one that would also help to lessen the possibility of terrorism today, would seem to be that of love, and loving service, and this forms the conclusion of his teaching in Mark 12.28–31. This means loving respect for the environment, for animals and the rest of creation; and, of course, for people.

Notes

1 *Sunday Times*, December the 1st, 2002.
2 Report by Helen Waterhouse and Tony Walter, entitled 'Reincarnation Belief and the Christian Churches' in *Theology*, January/February 2003.
3 The *Sunday Times*, December the 29th, 2002.
4 Report by Bruce Johnson in Rome; *Daily Telegraph*, September the 11th, 2001.
5 *The Times*, April the 20th, 2005.
6 Sermon Notes, the Jesuit Residence, at Farm Street Church, London Wl, for January the 12th, 2003.
7 Talk given by George Wood at the Theosophical Society, London, January the 30th, 2003.
8 *Baptist Times*, October the 31st, 2002.
9 *Sunday Times*, August the 11th, 2002.
10 Front page story by Edward Helmore in New York; *Observer*, London, March the 16th, 2003.
11 *Sunday Times*, November the 25th, 2001.
12 Article by Carsten Peter Thiede; *Church of England Newspaper*, December the 7th, 2001.
13 Talk given by John Michell, at a meeting of the Tenemos Academy at Essex Church, Notting Hill Gate, London, March the 5th 2003.
14 *Daily Telegraph*, September the 27th, 2005.
15 *Daily Telegraph*, January the 1st 2002.
16 Letter from the Education Officer of The Council of Christians and Jews, published in the *Church of England Newspaper*, December the 5th, 2002.

Bibliography

1 Addis, William and Arnold, Thomas, *A Catholic Dictionary*, Virtue & Co, 1925.
2 Batchelor, Mary, *Opening Up the Bible*, Lion Publishing, 1993.
3 Birks, Walter and Gilbert, R. A., *The Treasure of Montsegur – the Secret of the Cathars*, Thorsons, 1990.
4 Blakiston, Patrick, 'Reincarnation in Christian Thought'; a talk given to the Wrekin Trust, 1977.
5 Bridge, Anthony, *Theodora: Portrait in a Byzantine Landscape*, Cassell, 1978.
6 Brooke, George J., 'From Authority to Canon: Reworking the Bible at Qumran'; the Leonard Sainer Memorial Lecture given to the Institute of Jewish Studies at University College, London, January 2002.
7 Brown, Ray and Gillian with Dickson, Paul, *A Mere Grain of Sand*, Tagman Worldwide Ltd, 2004.
8 Catholic University of America, *The New Catholic Encyclopaedia*, 1967.
9 Cayce, Hugh Lynn (editor), *The Edgar Cayce Reader*, Volume II, Paperback Library, a division of Coronet Communications, USA; 1969.
10 Chadwick, Henry, *The Pelican History of the Church, Volume I: The Early Church*, Penguin Books, 1986.
11 'A Clergyman of the Church of England', *Reincarnation and Christianity*, William Rider, 1909.
12 Cowan, James, *Francis: A Saints Way*, Hodder & Stoughton, 2001.
13 Cross and Livingstone (editors), *A Dictionary of the Christian Church*, Oxford University Press, 1997.
14 Dibelius, Martin, A Fresh Approach to the New Testament and Early Christian Literature, Ivor Nicholson & Watson, London, 1937, and the International Library of Christian Knowledge.
15 Donfried, Karl P. (editor), *The Romans Debate*, Hendrickson Publishers, USA, 1991.
16 Duffy, Eamon, 'What about the Inquisition?' in *Priests and People*, January 1999.
17 Echlin, Edward P., *Earth Spirituality: Jesus at the Centre*, John Hunt Publishing, 2002.
18 Fisher, Joe, *The Case for Reincarnation*, Granada, 1984.
19 Gaskell, G. A., *The Dictionary of all Scriptures and Myths*, Grammercy Books, 1981.

20 Graham, Marilyn Grace, *On Reincarnation: the Gospel according to Paul: an interpretive matrix explaining Romans*, Quest Publishing, USA, 1998.

21 Guirdham, Arthur, *The Cathars and Reincarnation*, The C. W. Daniel Company Ltd, 1990.

22 Guirdham, Arthur, *The Lake and the Castle*, The C. W. Daniel Company Ltd, 1991.

23 Hall, Manly P., *Reincarnation: the cycle of necessity*, the Philosophical Research Society Inc., USA, 1939 (ninth printing, 1999).

24 Hamel, Christopher de, *The Book: a History of the Bible*, Phaidon, 2001.

25 Hamilton, Bernard, *The Christian World of the Middle Ages*, Sutton Publishing; 2003.

26 Hanson, Bradley C., *Introduction to Christian Theology*, Fortress Press, USA, 1997.

27 Head, Joseph and Cranston, S. L. (compilers and editors), *Reincarnation: an East-West Anthology*, The Julian Press, USA, 1961.

28 Head, Joseph and Cranston, S. L. (editors), *Reincarnation: The Phoenix Fire Mystery*, Julian Press / Crown Publishers Inc, USA, 1977.

29 Herklotts, Canon H. G. G., *How the Bible came to us*, Pelican Books, 1959.

30 Hick, John, *Death and Eternal Life* (section on 'Christianity and reincarnation'), Collins, 1976, and Macmillan, 1985.

31 Inge, Dean W. R., *The Platonic Tradition in English Religious Thought*, Longman, 1926.

32 Iverson, Jeffrey, *More Lives Than One? – The evidence of the remarkable Bloxham tapes*, Souvenir Press, 1976.

33 The King James Bible, Eyre and Spottiswoode Ltd, (Authorised Version – AV) London, Her Majesty's Printers.

34 Kung, Hans, *Eternal Life?*, sub-section entitled 'A Single or Several Lives?', SCM Press Ltd, reissued 1991.

35 Lane-Poole, Stanley, *Saladin*, Darf Books, 1985.

36 Langley, Noel, under the editorship of Hugh Lynn Cayce, *Edgar Cayce on Reincarnation*, Warner Books, 1967.

37 Leach, Charles, *Our Bible: how we got it*, Moody Press, USA, 1898.

38 MacGregor, Geddes, *Reincarnation in Christianity: a New Vision of the Role of Rebirth in Christian Thought*, Quest Books, USA, 1978.

39 MacGregor, Geddes, *Reincarnation as a Christian Hope*, MacMillan, 1982.

40 Mack, Burton L., *The Lost Gospel: the Book of Q and Christian Origins*, Element Books (first published in the USA by HarperCollins, 1993).

41 Mazzoleni, Don Mario, *A Catholic Priest meets Sai Baba*, Leela Press Inc, USA; 1994.

42 Montefiore, Hugh, *Looking Afresh: soundings in creative dissent*, SPCK, 2002.

43 Offwood, Donald, *Reincarnation and Christianity: our Spiritual Heritage*, Southern Lights, New Zealand, 1987.

44 Ouseley, G. J. R., *The Gospel of The Holy Twelve*, The Christian Gospel Trust, 1972 (seventh edition).

45 *Oxford Reference Encyclopaedia*, Oxford University Press; 1998.

46 Paston-Percy, *The Dictionary of National Biography* (Vol. XLIV), Smith Elder & Co, 1895.

47 Paul, N. M. (compiler), *True Stories from French History*, Griffith Farran Browne & Co Ltd, 1890.

48 Perry, Michael, 'Reincarnation – a Christian option?', *Epworth Review*, Volume 10, Number 2, May 1983.

49 Perry, Michael, *Psychical and Spiritual: Parapsychology in Christian faith and life*, The Churches' Fellowship for Psychical and Spiritual Studies, 2003.

50 Phipps, Peter, *Greater Than You Know*, Sathya Sai Publications, New Zealand, 1997.

51 Pixner, Bargil, OSB, *With Jesus through Galilee: according to the Fifth Gospel*, Corazin Publishing, 1992..

52 Ragg, Lonsdale and Laura (editors and translators), *The Gospel of Barnabas*, Hanif Publications. Originally published by the Clarendon Press and Oxford University Press, 1907.

53 Renwick, Timothy M., *Aquinas for Armchair Theologians*, Westminster John Knox Press, USA, 2002.

54 Richardson and Bowden (editors), *A New Dictionary of Christian Theology*, SCM, 1983.

55 Rieu, E. V. (translator), *The Four Gospels*, Penguin Classics, 1958.

56 Rosen, Steven, *The Reincarnation Controversy*, Torchlight publishing Inc, USA, 1997.

57 Rosher, Grace, *The Travellers Rest*, Psychic Press Ltd. 1965.

58 Stevenson, J. (editor), *A New Eusebius: documents illustrative of the history of the Church to AD 337*, SPCK, 1968.

59 Strong, Thomas, *Mystical Christianity*, Regency Press, 1978.

60 The Theosophical Society, *Reincarnation: A Christian Doctrine*, 1904.

61 Walsh, John Francis, *City of Gold*, Ecco Publishing, 1995.

62 Weatherhead, Kingsley, *Leslie Weatherhead: a personal portrait*, Hodder & Stoughton, 1975.

63 Weatherhead, Leslie D., *Life Begins at Death*, Denholm House Press, 1969.

64 Weatherhead, Leslie D., 'The Case for Reincarnation', a lecture given to the City Temple Literary Society, 1978.

65 Wheeler, Peter (compiler), *The Way of Love*, Leaders of the Way, 1995.

Where possible, attributions have been provided. In the event of omission, it is hoped that corrections can be made in a future edition.

Index

114

ACQUISITION/REVIEW
COPY N° 10

RS

16-10-2006